THE WAR WITHIN

To my late parents,
Solomon and Mercy,
who first pointed me to the Bible

THE WAR WITHIN

CHRISTIANS AND INNER CONFLICTS

A. C. Chukwuocha

HIPPOBOOKS

ACTS
Africa·Christian·TextbookS

Copyright © 2009 by A. C. Chukwuocha

Published 2009 by **Hippo Books**, an imprint of ACTS, Step, WordAlive and Zondervan.

Africa Christian Textbooks (ACTS), TCNN, PMB 2020, Bukuru 930008, Plateau State, Nigeria
www.africachristiantextbooks.com

Step Publishers, PO Box AN 11150, Accra-North, Ghana
www.stepbooks.org

WordAlive Publishers, PO Box 4547 GP0-00100, Nairobi, Kenya
www.wordalivepublishers.org

Zondervan, Grand Rapids, Michigan, USA 49530
www.zondervan.com

Library of Congress Cataloging-in-Publication Data

Chukwuocha, A. C.
    The war within : Christians and inner conflicts / A.C. Chukwuocha.
      p. cm. — (HippoBooks)
    Includes bibliographical references.
    ISBN 978-9966805393 (softcover)
    1. Christian life. 2. Conflict (Psychology) 3. Sin—Christianity. 4. Spiritual warfare. I. Title.
    BV4509.5.C48 2009
    248.4—dc22   w2009009948

Cover design: projectluz.mac.com
Book design: To a Tee Ltd, www.2at.com

09 10 11 12 13 14 15 • 15 14 13 12 11 10 9 8 7 6 5 4 3 2 1

CONTENTS

FOREWORD

I was reading a draft of this book on a flight from London to Lagos when I became aware that the young man sitting next to me was "giraffing", craning his neck to read it too. Suddenly aware that I had noticed what he was doing, he stopped reading and became rather pensive. Then he heaved a deep sigh. Was it of relief or frustration?

"May I disturb you, sir?" he asked.

"Certainly."

He felt assured. "Do you have this inner struggle yourself?"

"Yes, and I think most honest people would admit they do."

"And how do you gain victory in the situation?"

"I don't."

He was taken aback. Then I reassured him. "But God does. In fact he gained the victory long ago by the death and resurrection of Jesus Christ and by the gift of the Holy Spirit. So it is no longer my fight, but his; and it is no longer my victory, but his."

"You must have peace then – an inner sense of equilibrium, in spite of the possible tension." We both laughed.

"You must be an engineer or an architect – or even a surveyor."

"You are right, sir. But please, I need the answer to that question very badly – how can I really be the kind of Christian I am longing to be – or in your language, sir, how can I get the best from God?"

"Read this book," was my response.

The Rt. Rev. Cyril Okorocha
Bishop of Owerri
(Anglican Communion)

PREFACE

"Most honest people would admit they suffer inner conflicts," says the Rt. Rev. Cyril Okorocha. How is it that people who love to live right are sometimes drawn to do what is wrong? We know that many of the heroes in the Bible experienced this. Life appears to be full of inner tensions – the desire to do what is right is often offset by a pull to do what is wrong.

Young and old, great and small, everybody seems familiar with this conflict. We shout when we know we should keep calm, we watch when we should turn away, we move towards something we should be rejecting. On a more glaring level, we quarrel with our spouses, insist on getting our own way, enter into wrong relationships, lie, cheat and indulge illicit sexual desires. Or the struggle may involve getting up early to spend some time with God or getting a little more sleep, dealing with others respectfully or throwing our weight around, living up to our promises or finding reasons not to.

When we give in and do what is wrong, we get discouraged. If we are honest, we become frustrated and fear that we have abandoned our ideals. Some of us may even become so discouraged that we decide to quit living for Christ. Obviously, the issue of inner conflicts is a serious one.

What lies behind these inner conflicts Christians endure? Why do we have them when we are supposed to be holy? What is the normal Christian life really like? Are there Christians who live without these conflicts?

Even more importantly, do these conflicts jeopardize our salvation? Is it possible that they can make us lose our salvation? What if we give in to sin? What are the real results of sin in people's lives? And what about besetting sins? It is easy to label them as signs of demon possession, but is there any other way to see them? And how do we deal with them in practice?

We are told that the Holy Spirit can help us to live a holy life. But how do we ensure that we are filled with the Holy Spirit each day? Does listening to him mean that we don't need to use our minds? How can Christians live victoriously from day to day?

All these and more are questions that are addressed in this book. My aim in writing it is to answer them and to help believers to understand their salvation and live more fulfilled lives despite their inner conflicts.

It is my prayer that this book will be helpful in raising up a new army of stable and overcoming believers. May you be an answer to this prayer in the most high name of our Lord Jesus Christ. Amen!

A. C. Chukwuocha
Owerri, Nigeria
March 2009
christiansandinnerconflicts@yahoo.com

ACKNOWLEDGEMENTS

My special thanks go to the Rt. Rev. Cyril C. Okorocha for writing the foreword to this book and to Prof. Sam Olofin who read through the entire manuscript, offered useful suggestions and gave very keen support to this work.

Most Christian writers can only wish for the once-in a-lifetime opportunity of having Dr. John R. W. Stott read their work. I am short of words to express my gratitude to this exceptional servant of God for not only reading my work but also endorsing it. I also thank Dr. Chris Wright for introducing my work to Langham Literature.

I am indebted to Isobel Stevenson of Langham Literature for painstakingly going through the entire work over and over again to ensure the clarity of its message. I owe much gratitude to Krysia Lear who read through the challenging chapter on entangling sins and made very useful technical contributions.

Mr. and Mrs. Godwin Ekuma, Mr. and Mrs. Femi Adeleye and Mr. and Mrs. Sam Igbokwe represent a host of committed Christians who played varied important roles in getting this book published. Sir and Lady C. C. Chukwuocha and Mr. and Mrs. Emeka Chukwuocha represent the entire Chukwuocha family who supported the publishing of this work.

Lastly, without the support of my most beloved wife, Ngozi, this work might never have seen the light of day.

1

THE STRUGGLE WITHIN

My mind was racing. I had an appointment a few minutes away. I was not sure I could face it. I was just pulling out of the nightmare of two long days of tortuous counselling with Esla,[1] a young woman who insisted she was a Christian but had been accused of living in open sin. I had implored her to tell me the truth, and she had done exactly that. She had painstakingly narrated how for several years she had done her best to keep to the "holy path", but her attempts had brought her only continuous inner battles. She felt she was being crushed between two great mountains – the realities of her life and the expectations of her faith. Her final decision was what jolted me:

> I decided to remain a Christian. I can't deny Christ. The fact of my destiny without him is too clear to me. But I will no longer draw myself into those fanatical expectations that I can live clean like Jesus Christ. I trust that when Jesus comes he will wash me clean; for now, I can only be human.

Two months have passed and the nightmare of my failure to find a quick fix to Esla's problem is only beginning to fade away. Now I am in for another turn.

I sighed as my thoughts drifted to my present worries: "What if there are a number of others in our church with similar stories? What if everybody is like this, only pretending not to be?" Then I slipped into my deepest worry. Fred, one of our activity group leaders, had come in yesterday morning and calmly told me he had quit the faith. I managed

---

[1] Esla and Fred are fictitious names to protect the identity of real people.

to ask if it was because of the financial crunch he had been bearing for some time. "It's not that," he replied. "I think the Lord has really provided for me. The truth is that I am either an incurable sinner or I am not yet ripe for salvation."

I took a deep breath and tried to calm the cadence of my heartbeats and listen carefully. "The rate at which I get in and out of little sins is increasing by the day. My imaginations are mostly filthy. I get to envy easily. I lust for what should be shameful, and it is as if I cannot stop myself." I was astounded that he could say such things in the plainest language and felt totally unprepared to handle the situation. If he were sorrowful, I would have tried to calm him, encourage him and talk him back to faith. If he were boastful or lying, I would have rebuked him. But here he was, fully aware of being wrong, and yet with no real sense of guilt! I started pitying myself. How on earth was I to handle this situation again? My heart lifted to God for a moment. Then, I recalled my consciousness in time to catch what he was saying:

> Last night I woke up in the middle of the night. The entire place was dark and I remembered the mess I had slid into. I thought I should pray to God to help me out. But as I made to get out of bed, I noticed I was sandwiched between the wall and a woman. I wondered where I was. Then it hit me. I had wandered into a restaurant the previous night just to say hello. The proprietress was not in, and so the girl had served a variety of snacks, food and some drink. We went on to play cards and joke. My initial intention was to preach the word to her, but she was so warm in welcoming me and so excited that I came, that my resistance waned as I basked in the comfort and warmth of her company. Before I knew it, it was already far into the night and she persuaded me to stay. I sat up by the snoring girl wondering how I would explain this to my wife. At about four this morning I dashed home, only to lie to my wife that I had missed the last bus while we were praying with a troubled family.

He must have suspected my mind was wandering away again. Of course it was. I was wondering why he was filling me in on all these details, as if he were boasting of his exploits. He gave me a cold look:

I need a break. I am a disgrace. I can't teach in the church and live this way. I have fought frantically to stay afloat in the faith for quite some time now, but I get worse and worse. I suppose the best thing for me to do is to throw in the towel, go into the world, really try these things and keep on experiencing them till I begin to loathe them. Then I can stand without falling back.

What was the problem? Esla, too, had talked of this inner struggle to conform to holy living. She chose to accept worldly standards. Fred claimed to have initially fought to remain holy. Yet he finally failed. And that led to a worse situation. As though tethered to a boulder rolling into a ravine, he slipped from one problem to another in quick succession, and now talked as though he were lying at the bottom of the cliff in the shadow of death. Even if he had fallen into sin, why was his reaction to quit? My mind raced wildly through a forest of ideas.

I knew Fred fairly well, and one thing I knew about him was evident in the way he told his story. He was inclined to be smug. He must have been taught that there is room for forgiveness and cleansing if a Christian falls into sin. But Fred was the kind who would never accept that he had really made an A grade unless he scored 98 per cent. He was like Peter the apostle, confident in his own abilities. When Peter shared his opinion, he wanted everyone to believe it was a well-thought-out opinion. He was so confident that he even rebuked the Lord for his decision to go the way of the cross (Matt. 16:21–23). Jesus rejected that rebuke. Peter must have felt even more rebuffed when he saw his Lord arrested in Jerusalem. Jesus had predicted that Peter's pride would go before a fall (Luke 22:31–34). The feeble structures of his ego would be reduced to rubble. And he did indeed fall flat (Luke 22:54–60). The Lord's mighty hand humbled Peter so that he abandoned his efforts to rebuild that structure and clung to the Lord who was able to save his soul.

Perhaps Fred was passing through the same experience. His self-confidence must have informed his struggle to get clean and so please God, whereas he should have been flying to God for mercy. Who knows what a barrage of questions Fred must have asked himself? He had concluded he was unable to remain holy and must thus be rejected by God.

Fred's problem is in line with another one that should be of concern to many a church board: many potential candidates insist that they are not worthy to become ministers in the church or missionaries in other cultures. They regard being holy and not sinning as a prerequisite for ministry to others.

Their concern raises an even more profound question, one that was bothering Fred too. What does it mean to say that Jesus saves? Does receiving Jesus mean that he will actually prevent people from falling into sin? Does salvation have any appreciable effect in the present? Does it affect people's tendencies, character, conduct and general affairs? Are the lives saved completely redeemed in tangible terms from all defilement, accusations, and devil-propagated influences? What and how long does it take before believers become Christ-like?

The Bible states that "if anyone is in Christ, the new creation has come: The old has gone, the new is here!" (2 Cor. 5:17). Is the old order really completely gone? And is the new, in which only righteousness and the joy of holiness rule, come to us here on earth?

We see people embrace faith in Christ with great joy and enthusiasm. In the first few weeks after accepting the gospel, their old weaknesses and failures seem to have been jettisoned. They seem to have now found strength to overcome all the impediments that try to come between them and God. They are propelled with a new zeal and insist that "with God all things are possible". They tend to speak in absolute terms.

Unfortunately (and this is really unfortunate because it seems to apply to all Christians) soon after those early weeks in the faith, the "old" seems to creep back and begin to rear its ugly head. The deeply repentant become introspective and quiet down to find out what is going wrong. The more superficial continue with the outward noise and try to ignore or hide whatever is going wrong inwardly. Thus starts a lifelong struggle that has afflicted every Christian from Bible times till today. We all have to come to grips with some not-very-straightforward choices involving our faith.

Judas Iscariot endured this struggle and yielded to the strong temptation to choose money and betray Jesus. But once he had collected the money and the Lord had been led away and condemned by his enemies, the weight of his wrongdoing came upon him. He was presented with an even harder choice: to live and face his shame or to die. He forgot about God's mercy and chose to die (Matt. 26:14–16, 47–50; 27:1–5).

Peter's denial of the Lord came when he was forced to choose between risking his life by associating with the publicly rejected Jesus or saving his head for his wife. He denied Jesus in order to live. But thereafter he must also have been faced with the further choice of whether to continue on the path of denying Jesus. Guilt-stricken, he turned around and wept (Luke 22:54–62).

All the disciples ran away when Jesus was arrested to be crucified (Matt. 26:56). What inner shame must have stalked them when they were gathered in the upper room and the same Jesus they had deserted in trouble appeared and breathed upon them, "Peace!"

Paul, too, must have had inner struggles. When we read his words about the thorn that Satan sent to torment him (2 Cor. 12:1–10), do we stop to think what it must have been like for such a unique servant of Christ to have to struggle with something like this? He must have known inner conflict and been humbled and tempted to quit. Not even to mention the suffering he endured at the hands of the envious Jewish leaders. His nephew once brought news of a plot to kill him (Acts 23:12–22). That nephew and Paul's other relations were probably not yet Christians, and they must have put some pressure on Paul to withdraw from his collision course with the Jews. Quite some inner struggles!

All those who have walked with God were tempted like this. Abraham had to choose between God's demands and accepting the views and values of the world. He struggled with not having a son and had to choose between waiting on God and philandering with his housemaid. He tottered, choosing the latter, thereby creating a 13-year silence between God and himself (Gen. 16–17:2). Later on in life, when he had matured in the things of God through experiences of faltering and triumph, he took his only son to sacrifice him in obedience to God (Gen. 22). But not without an inner struggle!

The list keeps running: David struggled against taking another man's wife. He failed. He slipped further into murder to cover it up. God would not tolerate that! An inner struggle to humble himself to God before Nathan ensued. David made the right choice (2 Sam. 11–12:13).

He had earlier in life made a string of such right choices when he spared Saul's life (1 Sam. 24; 26) and honoured Mephibosheth, Jonathan's son (2 Sam. 9), yet none of these choices was made without a struggle.

Job struggled between loyalty to God and either accepting guilt for sins he had not committed or cursing God for causing him to suffer. He trusted in the righteousness of God and triumphed.

Moses, repeatedly tempted by the unfaithfulness of the Israelites, managed to live victoriously until he made one little choice: he failed to honour God with full obedience when he turned to rebuke the restive Jews and carelessly struck the rock instead of speaking to it. That "little" choice closed the door of his ministry, and he only saw but did not enter the land of promise. His earlier triumphs in his struggles could not save the situation. It was one failure too many (Num. 20:1–13; Deut. 3:23–28).

Even the Lord Jesus Christ suffered inner struggles. During his preparations for his ministry, he had to fight off the temptation to show his power "if" he was the Son of God. He was tempted to abandon the way of the cross and exchange the eternal glory that would bring for the painless, gregarious glory and honour of the kingdoms of this world (Luke 4:1–13).

A true walk with God is full of such experiences. Clearly, when one is in Christ, it is not only true that the "old things have passed away and the new has come" but also that part of the new that comes is this inner struggle to remain faithful!

The redemption story falls into two parts. The first part culminates in the second, which is the ultimate hope that we will be totally redeemed from sin, sorrow, pain and all evil and influences of the devil. We can be confident about this because heaven will contain only good and no evil, only God and no devil, only the Holy Spirit and souls made holy and no demons.

On the other hand, the first part of this redemption story has to do with the here and now on earth. Here, things are less clear-cut. The reason is that although God is in this world, so is the devil. Both the Holy Spirit and demons seek to influence human behaviour. There seem to be more people who do evil than there are people who do good. Those who are faithful are being made holy, but none of them is yet absolutely perfect.

So how far does Jesus save those who receive him now? Does he actually save here on earth? The Bible is right to say that the old has gone. But the new that has come is not unchallenged. The old has not been totally extinguished. Sometimes it wants to jump out of obscurity and superimpose itself on the new. The resulting struggle is one that all Christians of all generations have known. When Paul said, "I have fought the good fight" (2 Tim. 4:7) he was thinking of this struggle as a war. And a war it remains.

R. C. Sproul puts it this way:

> There still resides a corner of the soul that takes no delight in God. We see its ragged edge in our continued sin and we can observe it in our lethargic worship. It manifests itself even in our theology.[2]

It could even be said that the presence of inner conflicts may be a truer clue to whether one is saved than any claim to sinlessness or sinfulness. Our basic struggle on earth is to weaken the old and strengthen the new, until the new dominates in all areas of our lives.

My heart goes out to all those who have become disheartened because of the struggle of the old to regain control and rule their lives. Some have abandoned the faith, supposing that their sins have destroyed their relationship with God. Others may not have abandoned the faith but live in pain and distress, loathing themselves as lepers among the people of God. Still others have chosen an even more dangerous option. They have sold out their souls to their old nature. They call themselves Christians but engage in scandalous behaviour and wickedness without any remorse. Believing that the old can never really be subdued in any believer here on earth, they persist in sin and seek to maximize profit and pleasure, and yet they still hope to inherit the kingdom of God. They need to be reminded that "if we deliberately keep on sinning after we have received the knowledge of the truth, no sacrifice for sins is left, but only a fearful expectation of judgement and of raging fire that will consume the enemies of God" (Heb. 10:26–27).

What is really scary is not the struggle with the sinful nature but Christians' reactions to this struggle. These extreme reactions described

---

[2] R. C. Sproul, *The Holiness of God* (Illinois: Tyndale House, 1985), 231.

above are not so much the result of this struggle as of a lack of understanding of the relationship between our sinful nature and our salvation. It is the frustration of not matching preconceived ideas of what it means to be saved that makes people quit. Quit, yes, for to live outside this struggle is to live outside the faith. The Christian walk on earth exists only within the context of this struggle.

Preachers have sometimes aggravated the problem. The stronger their words and the more idealistic their message, the more likely it is that they are part of a generation too busy to really study the Bible. Some preachers tend to idealize the experience of the people of God here on earth and imply that their own experience has been ever so smooth. They fail to show how one can practically grow in holy living, clearing the hurdles. Their people struggle to live up to the message they have heard, but after ongoing struggles, some give up. They think that God did not accept them when they offered their lives to him. If he had, they assume that he would have empowered them to escape all the contradictions that daily confront them. Others assume that the reason they are struggling is that they are not serious enough about their faith.

There are even people who are discouraged from coming to Christ at all because of their sins. They think that they have to sort out their lives before they can come to Christ. But the Lord's invitation is to those who are "weary and burdened", those who need his rest (Matt. 11:28). If this is the case, why do some of those who struggle not trust Christ to eventually help them out? Some of those who remain in the faith despite their struggles never feel close enough to God to relate normally to him. They end up depending on "men of God" who they think are spared these struggles and intermittent failures. They become overly dependent. They do not really trust their faith. The entire spectrum of their lives becomes unhealthy. Their spiritual growth is stunted and their participation in the body of Christ creates more problems and nurtures such "little foxes" as envy, strife and gossip. As sin increases, instead of the church being edified, it decays and becomes more vulnerable to satanic attacks.

Those of us who continue in the faith know that what lies before us is a real struggle, a fight to the finish until we "escape this flesh", when we enter our final victory in Christ. But we also want an answer to the question of how we can emerge victorious from this struggle. Before we can even attempt to answer this question, we need to have a good understanding of what factors cause these inner conflicts and how to handle each of them.

Questions

1. What struggle does every Christian experience?
2. Do you experience any of this inner conflict? If so, describe your experience.
3. What is your attitude to this conflict?
4. What do you hope will happen to this conflict now and in the future? How do you expect things to change?

2

THE BASIC DYNAMICS OF INNER CONFLICTS

The causes of Christians' inner conflicts and frustrations are complex, but they are often related to a failure to understand some aspects of our faith. This chapter, therefore, focuses on making sure that we have a clear understanding of three important issues:

- Sin: what sin actually is and how it operates.
- Salvation: what salvation actually means.
- Temptation: the relationship between our spirit nature and our sinful nature.

Understanding Sin

Little Uka, frustrated in his attempts to move around to escape the hot afternoon sun, called out to his mother, "Mummy, please tell the sun to stop following me!" Sin, like the sun, keeps following us. Everywhere we go in this world, we see it. It is a troubling central issue in human life, and God is not prepared to play around with it. That is why Jesus came.

A person's name often tells you something about them. In Jesus' case, his name is a nutshell-description of his person, mission and ministry. His parents were told, "You are to give him the name Jesus, because he will save his people from their sins" (Matt. 1:21). The rest of the Bible confirms these words: "You know that he appeared so that he might take away our sins" (1 John 3:5) and "The reason the Son of God appeared was to destroy the devil's work" (1 John 3:8).

Theologians are convinced that all God's dealings with human beings since the fall are aimed at redeeming the entire human race from sin. The Bible starts with the book of Genesis. Genesis 1 and 2 talk about the creation of human beings. Genesis 3 describes how they fell into sin. Chapters 4 to 6:7 describe the chaos that resulted from their fall. Genesis 6:8 starts the story of the process by which God sets about redeeming us from the trouble of sin, and this redemption story runs from there on through the entire the Bible. In fact, the sixth to eighth chapters of Genesis can be seen as a symbolic demonstration of God's purpose. Only the first six verses of chapter 6 are used to show human wickedness. The next verse pronounces the punishment for that behaviour. Then from verse 8 on, all the verses up to the end of chapter 8 dwell on God's redemption of the human race through Noah. God's overarching aim is redemption. He does not want to condemn or judge, but to show mercy. As he told the prophet Hosea, "I desire mercy, not sacrifice" (Hos. 6:6).

The story of redemption as told in the Bible focuses on God's dealings with an individual, or a people, or the entire world. But all such dealings have one aim: that through them all the nations and peoples of the earth will ultimately be reconciled to God (Gen. 12:3; 2 Cor. 5:19). The Bible ends with the book of Revelation, which summarizes the redemption story and offers the hope of glory, the ultimate destiny of those God has redeemed.

Misunderstandings about Sin

Despite such a voluminous record, people do not seem to understand much about redemption from sin. Probably because of the vehemence with which God rejects sin and the description of the Son of God as the panacea for sin, some Christians think that once they receive Christ into their lives they will never sin again. By extension, if they again fall into sin, they think of themselves as lost, without any more hope. Some who brace up to continue in the faith after they have sinned presume that they have to begin all over again at the starting blocks of the race of faith. They think that their sin has made them fall out of Christ, and that they therefore need to come to Christ asking to be made children of God again. This is discouraging, not least because the one who fell thinks of the possibility of this cycle repeating itself continuously.

Misunderstanding of the nature of our sin and the redemption process is at the root of this lack of confidence in our salvation and, by extension, in the God of our salvation.

This problem of wrong reactions in the face of threatening sinfulness may look trivial, but it prevents people from growing in faith. Without a correct understanding of God and our relationship with him, dealing with sin is an impossibility. All anti-sin techniques that are not predicated upon a right understanding of our relationship with God will prove futile. The techniques may work for a few days or weeks, but the structure they build will soon cave in because its foundation is faulty; it was laid on the shifting ground of error. The only bridge that can bear the heavy load of our transformation from sinners to saints, from sinning to righteous living, is truth. That is why the Bible describes Jesus as "full of grace and truth" (John 1:14). The word "grace" speaks of God's sovereign intervention to count us who believe as righteous while processing us to be so rather than dealing out the condemnation we deserve. But the "truth" that is in Jesus helps us to truly understand God, his grace and his righteous demands. It helps us understand ourselves, our weaknesses and our need to escape from sin. Truth enables us to understand and follow the escape route from sin.

Many Christians fail to progress in their faith because they spend quality time pursuing imaginary issues instead of facing the real facts of their lives. Some who wrestle with besetting sins conclude that they were never saved, or that they are demonized. Some, like Fred in chapter 1, turn back from the faith and plunge into the world, hoping that they will return to the faith when they are more serious about it. They hope to escape from sin once they have had "enough" of it. This is a false hope because the natural person is never going to experience "enough" of sin. In fact the more one indulges in sin, the more one wants to sin.

Others, who locate the problem of sin in what they see and touch, start making rules, "Do not handle! Do not taste! Do not touch!" (Col. 2:21). The rules may convince them that they are breaking away from sin, but all too soon they are bewildered to find that they have fallen back into sin. As Paul said, "Such regulations indeed have an appearance of wisdom, with their self-imposed worship, their false humility and their harsh treatment of the body, but they lack any value in restraining sensual indulgence" (Col. 2:23).

Some time ago, I needed to pass a swimming test. As a child, I had been able to swim proficiently, but that was two decades in the past. I went to a trainer for well over three weeks, but with only a few days to go before the test, I still could not swim the length of the pool. I was worried and was blaming my failure on my stamina. So I started doing endurance exercises. But my trainer diagnosed my problem correctly: I had difficulty breathing out properly under water. We worked on my breathing for about thirty minutes, and soon I was swimming length after length without stopping. Watching me glide easily through the water, my trainer spoke with the voice of long experience: "It is not the amount of struggle that makes the difference; it's having the right technique."

The right techniques will get you swimming smoothly. Struggling produces lots of splashing and noise, but gets you nowhere. In the same way as I needed to learn the right techniques for swimming, so we need to learn God's techniques for overcoming sin. It is not a question of thrashing around in distracting struggles. We need to get to know God and to get to know who we are, with all our potential and frailties. Once we get to understand this and God's way of our salvation, we have made a good start on getting out of the quagmire of servitude to sin.

The Essence of Sin

When Adam and Eve sinned in Eden, the essence of their sin was not really that they ate the fruit. The real issue was their attitude to God that made them yield to the devil. This point is easier to appreciate if we imagine God saying to them at the moment of the temptation, "Remember what I told you, do not eat the fruit of this tree." Of course, they may not have heard the voice of God that day, just as we often do not when we are being tempted. But the reason was not that God was not there, nor that he did not speak. Rather, they had turned their back on God and were so focused on the object of their fancy that they did not hear God. In sinning we turn our backs on God; we turn away from him in desire for something else. And this is the essence of all sin.

When we sin we take God for granted. We make a statement of our independence from God and defiance of him. And Satan will use sin to try to keep us without God for life. This is the quintessential nature of sin. The prophet Isaiah aptly captured it when he wrote, "we all, like sheep, have gone astray, each of us has turned to our own way" (Isa. 53:6). It is in turning to our own ways of doing things that we sin. It is in living without recourse to God that we stray.

When we sin we follow the same steps as Adam and Eve when they sinned in Eden:

1. They desired the fruit: they focused on their own gratification instead of on pleasing God.
2. Satan embellished the evil to make it look good and thereby tempt them.
3. They turned their backs to God and ate the fruit, feeding the lower nature that loves sin and starving the spiritual nature that loves God.
4. Having been defiled by their sin, they fled from God, heading off in their own direction.
5. In keeping away from God, they were tossed like a rudderless ship in the destructive ocean of sin.

Our Sinful Nature and Our Spiritual Nature

In chapter 1, Esla complained she could not keep pure like Jesus. One of her problems was what to do about a local man called Captain. Captain had met Esla on her way back from the payphone booth and asked whether she lived in the neighbourhood. "Yes," she replied, "I'm a student at the university." Captain continued the conversation and ended by inviting her over to his room in a nearby hotel. He promised that in return he would give her some financial aid. Esla had actually gone to the phone to call her parents for the umpteenth time to send her money because she was broke. Would she accept Captain's offer?

When we make a choice, we exercise our God-given freewill. But our freewill does not operate in a vacuum. It is dependent on the information it receives from some other sources as we weigh the pros and cons in order to make a rational decision. And one item of information that we have to process is the one that distinguishes human decision-making from the choices made by beasts: we have to answer the moral question, "Is it right?" But morality is not an abstract thing. It must always have an object. For Christians, God is the source of all true moral values. It is in the light of God and his word that a moral decision may be said to be good or bad.

Before Adam and Eve ate the fruit in Eden they may have wondered what that fruit would taste like. Then they moved on to wondering why the Lord would not allow them eat it. Then came the next question, "What will happen if we eat it? Is it really poisonous enough to kill us?" But all the while these thoughts were passing through their minds, there must have been another thought pattern which kept cautioning, "Leave that fruit alone; it is not useful. Leave it alone; the Lord said we should not eat it." The two basic factors influencing human moral decisions are our sinful nature and our spiritual nature. These two express themselves through desires that contradict each other. Each attempts to influence our decisions. Our spiritual nature, also called our inner being or spirit, desires to please God. Our sinful nature, which Paul referred to as "the flesh", desires to gratify only itself. Describing this conflict, the Apostle Paul wrote, "For in my inner being I delight in God's law; but I see another law at work in me, waging war against the law of my mind and making me a prisoner of the law of sin at work within me" (Rom. 7:22–23).

When Adam and Eve sinned in Eden, their sin had two simultaneous results. First, their material senses were enhanced. The Bible says, "Then the eyes of both of them were opened, and they realized ..." (Gen. 3:7). What did they realize? They realized their material state. They saw that "they were naked". What they saw as bad was what God had seen as "very good", in harmony with their spiritual state (Gen. 1:31). So materially they sought to improve on what God had made them by making themselves coverings of fig leaves. The second result was that their spiritual sense was dimmed, "and they hid from the Lord God among the trees of the garden" (Gen. 3:8). While they became bold in the material sense, they became afraid in their inner being. Instead of drawing near to their maker in faith, they feared and fled (Gen. 3:8, 10).

It is important to notice a worrisome tendency. When their sin-tainted opinions contradicted God's, they felt enhanced. And this "enhancement" corrupted their spirits and made them hide from God. Their sinful nature became more influential than their now quite feeble and fearful spiritual nature, and thus human beings became prisoners to the desires of the flesh (Rom. 7:23).

As the sinful nature fed on sin through watching others sin and practising sin on its own, it got stronger in propagating more sin and became increasingly influential, sending sinful information and desires to our minds to influence our choices. Meanwhile our spirit nature starved, cut off from God, the only source of moral values and righteousness, and weakened more and more until it slipped into a coma. This was the state Paul says we were in before we received Christ. He describes it as being "dead in transgressions" (Eph. 2:5). In other words, we had become insensitive to real life. Our unresponsiveness to the spirit life and righteousness is equivalent to spiritual death. The only faculty that was really active was our lower nature, which is so corrupt that it is essentially sinful, and is thus called our sinful nature.

The spirit had been so weakened that even though it sometimes expresses a desire for righteousness, it lacked the ability to persuade our will to act against the desire of the flesh (Rom. 7:18). It needs external help if it is to rise again. And that is one good reason why the man from heaven had to come to save us. None of us could deliver ourselves, just as an animal caught in a trap cannot set itself free or help another trapped animal. We have all been trapped and imprisoned by our sinful nature.

We thus learn from Scripture a number of lessons about the state we fell into when we sinned and about the way out of it:

1. Our sinful human nature (the flesh) contains nothing good (Rom. 7:18). It has been totally corrupted.

2. The human spirit is willing to engage in prayer (Matt. 26:41) and be obedient to God (Rom. 7:22), but it is too weak to do what it wants to do. It also faces active opposition from our sinful nature.

3. Our sinful nature (flesh) is irredeemably corrupted; what is redeemed is our inner being. In 1 Corinthians 5:5 the Bible recommends punishment for an immoral Christian "for the destruction of the sinful nature so that his spirit may be saved on the day of the Lord". No matter what is done, our sinful nature will ultimately be destroyed.

4. We are saved when the Holy Spirit raises our spirit nature and enables it to grow in strength (Eph. 3:16). The Spirit will work to continually

weaken the flesh so that its desires will lack the force to determine our choices. As Scripture says, "If Christ is in you, your body is dead because of sin, yet your spirit is alive because of righteousness" (Rom. 8:10 NIV). Thus we see that in a believer, the flesh still inclines to sin, but since we no longer give in to sin, the flesh begins to die. But the spirit is now alive and healthy because the believer now lives in righteousness, and thus nourishes it.

5. Since it is the Holy Spirit that nurtures our spirit, the struggle between our sinful nature and our spirit is also a struggle between our sinful nature and the Holy Spirit (Gal. 5:17).

6. We can become stronger in righteous living by sowing to the Spirit, that is, by cultivating the right atmosphere for the Holy Spirit to work in through studying the word of God, praying and interacting with other Christians who encourage us to live in obedience to the Holy Spirit. If we neglect these things, we are allowing an atmosphere to develop that will arouse the flesh, particularly if we keep unedifying company. Strengthening the flesh leaves us more susceptible to sin and destruction (Gal. 6:8).

Paul tells us that "the sinful nature desires what is contrary to the Spirit and the Spirit what is contrary to the sinful nature. They are in conflict with each other" (Gal. 5:17). This inner struggle will last our lifetime here on earth.

Understanding Salvation

When we are saved, we are reconciled with God. What happens to us practically is that our spirit – our righteous inner being – is raised from the coma it slid into when we sinned and turned our backs on God. Our spirit is now attached to the life-supporting Holy Spirit.

If turning from God to our own ways is the core of sin, then salvation involves the exact opposite. Instead of turning our backs on God and defiantly choosing to sin and be estranged from him, we turn around to face God and submit to him. Being saved will lead us to develop a heart of obedience to God, always eager to please him, and so lead to us doing individual acts of righteousness.

When the Bible says that Jesus will save his people from their sins, we at times assume that it means that when we accept Christ he destroys the sinful nature and will prevent us from sinning again. But that is not the case. Rather, salvation reverses the order by which we strayed into sin:

1. The Holy Spirit turns us back to God through the knowledge of Jesus Christ and belief in him.

2. We now focus on God and our spiritual nature is nourished by the Holy Spirit while our sinful nature is starved.

3. The word of God reveals the truth to us progressively and rescues us from the lies of the devil that held us in bondage.

4. As we experience God's love and truth, we desire to know him more and more. Instead of seeking sinful gratification, we seek to draw nearer to God.

5. As we stay in God, we are also kept from sin.

Because we are all rightly bothered by the volume of sin that floods this world, we would prefer it if Jesus instantaneously and absolutely wiped away sin from people's lives when they were saved. So we often act as if the only way people can prove that they have been saved is by being sinless. In the same way, the Jews of old insisted that the only proof that someone was truly the Messiah would be the political emancipation of Israel. Both we and the Jews are right – up to a point. But both of us are looking too far into the future. Our becoming sinless and the deliverance of the Jews will come – but not immediately.

The main thing God does for us when he saves us is to deliver us from his wrath by restoring us to relationship with himself through Jesus Christ. Our guilt is cancelled. This action is called justification and it establishes us as beloved children of God. The Apostle Paul stressed this truth when he declared: "There is now no condemnation for those who are in Christ Jesus" (Rom. 8:1). Justification is the prerequisite for the process of sanctification, which makes us holy in character.

The restoration of our relationship with God also has other consequences. We now have a responsibility to please God, to meet his love for us with our love for him. We did not care about these things in the past, when we were unsaved enemies of God. But if we sincerely love and honour him, we will be like the Apostle Paul and "make it our goal to please him" (2 Cor. 5:9).

In order of precedence, the agenda of God in saving us through Jesus is first to restore us to himself, save us from his wrath and cancel our guilt. Secondly it is to help us obey him by the Holy Spirit so that we may enjoy our relationship with him. Thirdly, it is to teach us the fruitlessness and death that come by sin so that we will willingly resist sin in our struggles and thus "prosper and be in health". We may fail at times, but God's programme is still to cleanse us and get us to move forward.

Jesus saves those who believe in him by making them trust in God and receive Christ's righteousness, which delivers them from the wrath of God. But Jesus does not manipulate the way things are in this world to shield his own from being tempted. His believers are still affected by the failures and decay of the world. But in the midst of these failures, they are called to be salt, to season the world and prevent decay; surrounded by the darkness of sin, they are called to bring light to the world.

Because God knew that believers would sometimes fail, he included confession, forgiveness, cleansing and restoration as integral components of the new covenant in Christ Jesus. This in itself is significant evidence of the nature of salvation. We are only justified sinners; we are not yet glorified saints.

Understanding Temptation

The Apostle James showed a clear understanding of the intricacies of temptation when he wrote, "Each of you is tempted when you are dragged away by your own evil desire and enticed" (James 1:14). He identifies the two basic factors that work together: our desire and the tempter's offer to fulfil that desire. One of these factors is inherent in us: Satan does not tempt anyone with what they do not desire or fancy. It is not common to catch 98-year-old women committing adultery! The other is only a welcome guest: Satan cannot break into our lives if we keep away from him by keeping to God's truth.

Even when our desires are legitimate, the devil will offer us easier, but illegitimate, ways of fulfilling them, thereby making the desires evil. And sometimes the devil kick-starts the process by presenting us with opportunities that appeal to our habitual fantasies and so creates desire. Satan may also overwhelm us with issues we have not yet learnt how to handle or with an issue we have not outgrown. Thus desire is produced, and the entire vicious circle is repeated. Through temptation, Satan draws us to stray from God and turn to our own ways.

Earlier in this chapter I explained that our sinful desires come from the sinful nature that influences our choices. The devil and his cronies charm our minds by embellishing those desires, making them captivating in order to take us captive. They tempt us to fulfil evil desires in a way that make it very difficult for us to offer any resistance to full-blown temptation.

What then is this temptation? It is that drawing away of one's mind from the truth, and the charming of one's mind to pursue a course that is unpleasant to God. It is also the embellishing of evil, enticing our mind through filling it with ideas of the benefits of indulging our desires. Temptation is also the whetting of the appetite for real or imaginary gratification.

During temptation the devil does a lot to ensure that our minds are upset in order to keep us from hearing from God. In Eden, God's voice of caution must have been drowned out and awareness of his presence dimmed by the fascination of the possibility of tasting this desired fruit, by the excitement of experiencing this one "thrill" that had eluded them. Their minds were carried away by Satan's temptation and the irresistible allure of the fruit. It did not matter that the fruit might be bitter. Satan had whetted their desire by presenting the fruit as full of fun, excitement and magic – the magic that would transform them to become "like God". For us, the thunderous call to enjoy the "fruit" drowns out the "still small voice" of God's caution. We are certain of the pleasure that will come from indulging the desire, and gloss over any possibility of suffering for the indulgence. But the truth about sin is that while indulgence may be momentarily pleasurable, its eventual cost is very high. The price paid for sin will always outweigh the value derived from it.

The modern equivalent of Eve's desire for the fruit could be a young man's lust for property or a woman's quest for another's husband. It could be someone's desire to achieve fame at any price. It could be another's quest to assert themselves over others. All of these desires have one thing in common: they involve insubordination to God. They are the assertion of self against the sovereignty of God, the author and sustainer of all life.

Scripture seems to indicate that temptation has some power to coerce us into sinning. The Lord Jesus twice tells us to pray against temptation. In the Lord's Prayer, we are instructed to pray, "Lead us not into temptation" (Matt. 6:13), and in Gethsemane Jesus told his disciples to "watch and pray so that you will not fall into temptation" (Matt. 26:41). One would have expected the Master to care more about actual sin rather than merely temptation to sin, but his concern shows that we are better off without temptations, and should do our best to avoid being entangled by them.

When We Are Vulnerable

Temptation comes using every weapon in the devil's armoury. Most of the time, it comes when we are somewhat off-balance emotionally, mentally or even psychologically, and the lack of balance makes it very easy to stumble and fall. Thus anger can lead some people to speak destructive words, or even to kill. Fear causes others to succumb. That was what happened to the Apostle Peter, who denied his Master very shortly after a notable act of bravery in defending him (Matt. 26:47–54, 69–75). Elijah, too, gave in to fear when he closed his rising ministry because Jezebel had threatened to kill him (1 Kings 19:1–5). Yet he had previously brought about one of the strongest revivals in the history of Israel. Similarly, some pastors confess that they did not know what force came over them when their hearts were charmed by a woman who came for counselling.

In the face of overwhelming temptation, people can feel somewhat tipsy, with their senses either dulled or heightened, and their minds agitated, depressed or forgetful. Those were some of the signs that God saw in Cain just before he murdered Abel: "The Lord said to Cain, 'Why are you angry? Why is your face downcast? … Sin is crouching at your door; it desires to have you, but you must rule over it'" (Gen. 4:6–7). In luring Cain towards the sin of murder, Satan first agitated his mind with anger and depression. Emotions like this work on our minds until we are "drunk" on emotion and in a moment of utter misjudgement fall flat before the temptation. When God saw anger and depression in

Cain, he knew that his emotional disposition would slide him straight into sin. So he instructed Cain to master the temptation and avoid the sin. We would do well to recognize these early signs of temptation and sin from afar and do away with them as soon as we see them.

In moments of great excitement, people have made statements that ruined them for life. Herod was so excited by Herodias' daughter's dance at his birthday party that he made an offer that got him to regretfully behead John the Baptist (Matt. 14:6–10). A young man whose wedding banquet was held in a five-star hotel was so caught up in the excitement that he announced over the loudspeakers that the waiters should serve people whatever they wanted. The first years of his marriage were blighted by the stress of paying the resulting bill, which necessitated selling a lot of his property and borrowing from others.

Some people, especially those who live without recourse to the Lord Jesus Christ, live with emotional instability and are filled with anger, bitterness, shame, anxiety, fear, unforgiveness, hatred, envy, lust and so on. Such people are prone to a range of temptations. Their spouses are often very unhappy. Simple issues that other families handle calmly create more and more trouble for them. Reading this, some of you may shout, "Yes! That is why I have to end it all. I want a divorce!" That is falling for another temptation. The problem is not necessarily your spouse. Try and be happy and tolerate your spouse's shortcomings as you do your own, and watch your spouse improve simply because he or she is accepted. Christians, too, are in danger if they do not allow the Holy Spirit to control their emotions through the word of God. Churches are also in danger when the leadership is autocratic and the members are not given avenues to express their feelings. When feelings of frustration run high, there will be a harvest of evil ranging from gossip to subversion.

We can now see why people who are generally unhappy, people with insecure, egocentric, proud or ambitious mindsets, or even people who are overly excited are prone to falling for one kind of temptation or another. Of course, it is not only those whose circumstances keep them emotionally unstable who are tempted – they are simply more prone to temptation. All of us, however, are tempted in various ways. If we live in emotionally stable conditions, Satan will be lurking around for moments when our emotions are a bit off-control, or he will create such moments by helping us to become too busy to have time to think clearly, or by some other tactic.

It is for the above reasons that Jesus warned us, "Be careful, or your hearts will be weighed down with dissipation, drunkenness and the anxieties of life" (Luke 21:34). We are also cautioned in several places to watch our emotions. The Lord said to Joshua, "Do not be afraid; do not be discouraged" (Josh. 1:9). Jesus said, "Do not worry" (Matt. 6:25). Paul wrote, "Do not be anxious about anything" (Phil. 4:6). The psalmist wrote, "Refrain from anger and turn from wrath; do not fret – it leads only to evil" (Ps. 37:8). Paul wrote, "Keep your head in all situations" (2 Tim. 4:5). If we are going to avoid unnecessary temptations, it will be by keeping our heads.

This is why the Apostle Peter calls on us to be always clear minded, self-controlled and alert, that is to say, emotionally stable, so that we can pray (1 Pet. 4:7, 5:8). He talks of prayer as having the potential to keep us emotionally, psychologically and spiritually stable. This stability, which comes from real communication with God and faith in him, gives us the necessary poise to either avoid or overcome temptations.

Why Satan Tempts Us

Satan tempts us by latching onto the weaknesses of our flesh or our natural desires and using them to seduce, intimidate, incite or confuse us into doing the wrong thing or doing right things the wrong way. Sometimes he lures us to satisfy legitimate desires by doing the wrong things. He does this for a number of reasons.

- **He wants to create trouble in our lives:** Satan's aim is to prevent us from enjoying peace, and so he creates tension in couples, neighbours, and other relationships. It is his joy to see human beings, created in God's image, filled with sorrow and pain, and so he uses sin to bring trouble into our lives, whether we are believers or unbelievers. In chapter 6 we will consider a number of lives that Satan has messed up through sin in Bible times and in our own days.

- **He wants to keep us from being saved:** In tempting people who are not yet saved, Satan aims to keep them from ever coming to Christ. He blackmails people with the threat that they will suffer shame or pain if they repent. Sinful ambitions, desires and memories of old sins can discourage us from turning from old ways to be saved by Christ. Satan may also deceive us into thinking that we cannot do without sin, and he can help people explain away their sins by giving reasons for them. He thus keeps people in their sin, away from Christ. Satan also often makes people despise the preacher, dub him a hypocrite, and imagine that he could never be better than they are. His aim is to lead people on from one sin to another until he entraps them in situations that are very difficult to break away from. For example, he may encourage some people to become good churchgoers, people whom others praise for their usefulness in the church, but who have not personally and practically reconciled with God, breaking away in repentance from their past. Such people think of sin in universal terms – "everyone sins" – but never face up to their individual failure – "I have sinned". They are deceived into imagining that they will be saved alongside all others who manage to do some good. They never see any reason to repent of *who they are*; they think more of *whatever little good they now do*. They are a prime example of how Satan tempts us to keep us from ever being saved.

- **He wants to make us unproductive:** If Satan can get us to sin, he weakens our witness for Christ and thus our capacity to influence others for Christ. When we fall, he responds by making us either stop talking about Christ or do even more illegitimate things to cover up our sin – and then he uses these things to destroy our ministry or witness for Christ. If he cannot get us actively involved in sin, he will try to keep us occupied with trifles, church politics, or other things which distract us from our calling and make us less productive in ministry.

- **He wants to discourage us:** Satan likes to make us doubt our salvation and thus our relationship with God. This doubt produces a harvest of evil. It deprives us of the confidence to come near God to ask him for help or to trust him for our good. Thus if Satan can get us to sin, he will use our failure to fight our faith and get us off balance so that we stumble further and become discouraged. He gnaws away at our faith.

- **He wants to make us quit:** Satan may so deepen the doubt he creates in us as a result of sin that we begin to feel like quitting the faith. He does his best to convince us that we are not good enough because we sin, or that our continued failure to reach Christ's standards means that we are not really children of God.

Satan's temptations range from very simple to highly complex ones, which may not be easy to handle once given in to. We must therefore seek to strengthen our faith so that we have the advantage in these inner conflicts.

How We Are Vulnerable

One mistaken idea that appears prevalent among Christians is that when we are saved our sinful nature is destroyed. In the course of writing this book I have encountered a number of Christians who expressed shock at realizing that the sinful nature was still alive in them. One brother claimed we are called to mortify the flesh, whereas what we are actually told to do is to "mortify the deeds of the body" (Rom. 8:13 KJV). Another reminded me of Romans 6:6, which the King James Version of the Bible renders, "Knowing this, that our old man is crucified with him, that the body of sin might be destroyed, that henceforth we should not serve sin." These words led this dear brother to believe that the old sinful nature is dead in a believer. But when we look at the New International Version's translation of this verse, it reads, "so that the body of sin might be done away with" (or "be made powerless" – NIV footnote). The Living Bible makes it even clearer: "Your old evil desires were nailed to the cross with him; that part of you that loves to sin was crushed and fatally wounded, so that your sin-loving body is no longer under sin's control, no longer needs to be a slave to sin;" The sinful nature is crushed, fatally wounded, and rendered powerless, but it is not yet dead.

Other passages in the Bible reveal that the sinful nature is still alive, but not well, in a believer. Galatians 5:16–17 reads, "So I say, walk by the Spirit, and you will not gratify the desires of the sinful nature. For the sinful nature desires what is contrary to the Spirit, and the Spirit what is contrary to the sinful nature. They are in conflict with each other, so that you are not to do whatever you want." A sinful nature which still desires and is still in conflict is not yet dead. It is alive, but you are at liberty to weaken it by denying its desires. You can weaken it till it goes into a coma and becomes ineffective in your life, but it will not die until you die. Remember that the devil prefers you to assume that the sinful nature, the enemy within, is dead, so that you will be taken unawares when he attacks.

Two major problems stem from the mindset that says that the sinful nature is dead. The first is that, if this were true, people could claim to be already perfect and without sin. They could insist that they are immune to temptation because there is nothing left in them that is receptive to anything sinful. The problems created by this first idea are visible in many of today's Christian heroes. Their humanity and frailty are all too obvious, but rather than admit their weakness, as Paul did in 2 Corinthians 12:7–10, they excuse their sinful acts and try to make them appear righteous. They need to prove that the assumed result of Jesus' death is fulfilled in their lives, and so they insist that "the man of God does not sin". This assumption leaves no room for true repentance for sins.

The second major problem is also in evidence today. There are those who insist that because the sinful nature in a believer is dead, believers are invulnerable to temptation and need take no precautions against sin. Thus some preachers arrange private live-porn sessions, hoping nothing will go wrong. Some Christian counsellors innocently design their counselling rooms as more or less secret rooms, and take people of the opposite gender there for counselling sessions. Some pastors feel strong enough to keep the church's funds or even to accept members' money for safekeeping, sometimes without even paper records. They trust that neither they nor their brethren can be tempted since, as they suppose, the sinful nature is dead. They are insulted if we ask for paper records of transactions with fellow believers, or when we confirm the actual amount of money we received when fellow believers pay us. Our actions are interpreted as casting doubt on the other believer's salvation, rather than as an effort to undermine an inherent and common enemy. The reason again is that they do not want to believe that the sinful nature is alive in a believer.

Before we were saved, our sinful nature was fully in control of us, without any effective opposition. We were all prisoners of the desires of the sinful nature. Our spirit nature, the inner being was in a coma, poisoned by sin and starved because of the severed link to God. The Holy Spirit started to bring healing by arousing us from this coma when we repented and were justified, being accepted again by God. As we rely more and more on the Holy Spirit, our inner being is energized and grows to be stronger and more influential than the sinful nature, which is being poisoned by the life of God in us. The inner being thus comes to influence our lives more than the old sinful nature. We can see evidence of this in the opinions of believers that express their inner thoughts – their love for God and their love and tolerance for others. But this does not mean that the sinful nature is dead, it is only weakened and relegated to obscurity. We need to remember the words of C. Donald Cole, "People are different, and circumstances are different. But we are alike in that we all fail, and we fail for the same basic reason: we are still sinners."[1] In saying we are still sinners he means that the sinful nature still inhabits each and every one of us, and is operative in differing degrees. "The old, sinful nature will not die until our bodies die. Not until we expire will we cease to feel the force of temptation."[2] "As long as you live your lower nature will be around to tempt you."[3] This is why we sin.

The Inevitable Conflict

When the sinful nature ruled in us, our lives were about sin all the way. Jesus came and woke up our inner being, our spirits, and now that righteous spirit contradicts the sinful nature. When the sinful nature desires to use parts of my person for sin, my spirit contends with it. When my spirit desires to do righteousness, the sinful nature struggles to quench the righteousness.

There is a war going on within me. Whichever of the two factors is better equipped for each battle wins. So I need to equip my spirit by constantly nurturing it by the Holy Spirit, the word of God and prayer. I weaken the flesh by denying it the nourishment of sin and selfish desires and indulgences. Many of the battles I will experience are about my priorities as I shift my values from esteeming material things and desiring human honour to desiring things of eternal value, and supremely the knowledge of Christ.

---

[1] C. Donald Cole, *How to Know You are Saved* (Chicago: Moody Press, 1988), 46.
[2] Ibid., 51.
[3] Bill Perkins, *Fatal Attractions* (Oregon: Harvest House, 1991), 135.

Questions

1. How does the author describe the nature of sin?
2. Through what does our sinful nature operate?
3. Can you identify desires you have that are sinful?
4. What is the conflict in you?
5. How do you think this inner conflict came about?
6. What is temptation?
7. What are Satan's aims in tempting you?
8. What provisions has God made for you to overcome temptations?
9. How do you plan to let righteousness win daily in you?

3

THE HOLINESS QUESTION

A mob of angry villagers armed with clubs, torches and machetes scoured the forest searching for the driver whose car had knocked down a boy some half-hour earlier. The boy had dashed into the road from a nearby bush while chasing after a squirrel. One thing was certain; if they caught the driver he would be dead. His car was already ablaze. After long hours of search, they trooped back, trotting in from the different directions in which they had been dispatched to cordon off the area of bush the driver had run into. The driver had escaped into police custody six miles away. The villagers chanted and yodelled, convinced that the police would execute him for murder. I sighed in relief. The man was safe, safer than he would have been if he had tried to escape from the police; safer than he would have been if he had fallen into the hands of the mob.

Someone reading what we have written so far may feel that I am overstressing the continuing role of sin and remind me that Christians are called to holy living. True, the normal Christian life is a holy one, anything else is abnormal. But this book is written to answer the question, "How should we react if we do sin?" This is the same question that the Apostle John was dealing with when he wrote, "My dear children, I write this to you so that you will not sin. But if anybody does sin, we have an advocate with the Father – Jesus Christ, the Righteous One. He is the atoning sacrifice for our sins, and not only for ours but also for the sins of the whole world" (1 John 2:1–2). Just as the police advise you to be careful on the road, but if you do have an accident, report it to them, so John says that we should not sin, but if we do, we should go to Jesus. Jesus is far better than the police. The police will protect you from the mob, but will still prosecute you. Jesus will deal with the consequences of your sin, for he is "faithful and just and will forgive us our sins and purify us from all unrighteousness" (1 John 1:9).

But the reader may insist, "I want to be holy, constantly enjoying a victorious life and not just being satisfied with confessing my sins. How can I become holy? How can I overcome the daily inner conflicts and temptations of this life?"

To be able to answer that question, we first need to understand the concept of holiness.

A Common View

The first time I read a book by J. I. Packer, I felt I was learning theology in an arithmetic class! The clear-minded theologian constantly used expressions that are like the mathematical "equals", "therefore", "equivalent to", and so on. It was fun following his line of argument and yet also demanding to plunge in to study using his incisive method. But the experience was well worth it: I left that class with a strong impression that the Bible is true and that it is to be honoured as the word of God that is relevant to all generations, including ours. Packer's confidence in probing the word somehow rubbed off on me.

While I cannot write like J. I. Packer, I will imitate him in taking a disciplined and scholarly approach to answering the question of what it means for a human being to be holy. Thus I will begin by asking whether a human being can be holy in the same way as God is holy. "Holy" is the word used to describe the quality and state of character of God and all that he does. He is holy! Surely he must be the standard by which we judge holiness?

This argument seems plausible, but it does not hold up for very long. Even though we may be seen as holy if we act as God does, there are times when we can become unholy by doing some things that God does! For instance, Scripture says, "our anger does not produce the righteousness that God desires" (James 1:20). Yet, obviously, the anger of God works the righteousness of God. In fact God's anger is a characteristic that points to his holiness. It shows that he is opposed to evil.

The statement that "God is holy" assumes, rightly, that God is perfect. While "holy" describes the quality of everything about God, "perfect" fixes the state of this holiness. It is complete, wanting nothing in quality or quantity. Nothing can be added to or removed from God's holiness in order to improve it. God can neither be built up nor destroyed. He will not change his state. Even though he could do this, he has chosen not to. Yet God did the unexpected when he took on human flesh in Jesus Christ. He accepted and suffered human emotional failures. He was tired and often hungry. The ultimate in glory, he suffered shame. Yet the one thing he refused to give up was his holy state. He would not become sinful. The personality of God abhors, repels and even expels sin. God is incompatible with sin.

Compared to God, no one is holy! The level of God's holiness is far beyond anything a mere human could achieve. To underline this point, we need look no further than James 1:13: "God cannot be tempted". The same cannot be said of us.

So what then does it mean to say that we must be holy? All holiness must emanate from obedience to God. The holiness of God lies in the fact that God remains obedient to himself. This statement must not be misunderstood to mean that at some initial time God created a set of rules that he keeps obeying today to remain holy. That idea has two fundamental flaws. One, God has no "initial time". He has neither beginning nor an end; he is from everlasting to everlasting. His nature is not dated, ruled or regulated by time. Secondly, this idea would suggest that there are two gods. The first one was more powerful, and set rules for the latter to obey. Such theology is wholly strange to the Bible and the God of the Bible.

When we say that God obeys himself, what we mean is that God remains true to his own nature. In declaring his name, "I am", to Moses (Exod. 3:14), God was revealing that he does not change. There is no "was not" or "will be" with God. He is perfect! He is what he is; in every sense. His will is his will, and it is the same yesterday, today and forever. Our yesterday, today and tomorrow are all contained in God's eternal now.

Jesus' clear understanding of this led to his abiding "grammatical error", when he compared the eternal God and human beings, saying, "before Abraham was born, I am" (John 8:58). He was claiming "to have been existing eternally before Abraham."[1]

---

[1] John R. W. Stott, *Basic Christianity* (Illinois: InterVarsity Press, 1971), 28.

In Jeremiah 9:24, God declares that holiness is his abiding characteristic: "I am the Lord, who exercises kindness, justice and righteousness on earth, for in these I delight." God continues to delight in these. He is the "I am", and what he liked in the past, he likes now, and will continue to like. Whatever he hated in the past, he still hates and will continue to hate." His state of holiness will not change.

Human beings, on the other hand, can become holy by living in accordance with their creator's pattern for right living, or in other words, in accordance with the revealed word of God. Dr. D. M. Lloyd-Jones is quoted as observing that, "Holiness is not an experience you have; holiness is keeping the law of God."[2]

Someone who is holy is someone who lives in obedience to God. Such a person must withdraw from everything that goes against God's word and engage only in things that please God. Too often, we think that people are holy because we see them avoid things that are wrong. This is rather an incomplete and unfortunate assessment emanating from the recurring misunderstanding of holiness. Someone who is holy does not just avoid unrighteousness, he or she must also actively (and not merely passively) practise righteousness and engage in good works.

But there is a catch that we still need to consider. God is holy because he has remained absolutely free of sin. He has never been stained by or inclined to sin. So no matter from which angle we talk of God, we cannot find a "but" attached to his holiness. On the other hand, human beings have been fallen since Adam and Eve sinned. Our stories are like that of the impressive Aramite army officer, Naaman. After all his credentials had been marshalled, the description of him ends with the words, "but he had leprosy" (2 Kgs. 5:1). All his achievements are tainted by this "but". Even if someone managed to be so reformed that he or she does not sin any more, the record of their life will still contain the line, "but he was a sinner". How can we ever wipe this "but" out of our record?

Once again, our views about holiness have run into a dead end. If we expect people to be declared holy because they have achieved purity, we will face continual frustration and will end up asking with Job: "But how can mere mortals prove their innocence before God?" (Job 9:2).

---

[2] Richard Alderson, *No Holiness, No Heaven* (Edinburgh: The Banner of Truth Trust, 1986), 30.

What is wrong is not our expectation that human beings can be holy. No! What is wrong is our approach to human holiness.

Some believe that they will achieve holiness when they reach the point where they are so pure that they escape the inner struggles. They hope that by being born again their sinful nature will die and that they will never again be drawn to "a very high mountain" where they will be tempted by the "kingdoms of this world". However, this is not God's approach to helping us overcome the flesh and become holy.

A Separated Life

Each time we think about holiness from the point of view of what we can achieve in this life, we are mistaken. Our private efforts to become holy are a failure. We do not have the capacity to achieve holiness. This point is driven home even more when we read R. C. Sproul's discussion of what "holy" means:

> The primary meaning of 'holy' is 'separate' … To translate this basic meaning into contemporary language would be to use the phrase 'a cut apart' … 'a cut above something … '
> When the Bible calls God holy it means primarily that God is transcendentally separate. He is so far above and beyond us that he seems almost totally foreign to us. To be holy is to be 'other', to be different in a special way.[3]

This idea is demonstrated in Hebrews 7:26, which talks of Jesus as "one who is holy, blameless, pure, set apart from sinners, exalted above the heavens." God has the same opinion of himself. He told his people: "As the heavens are higher than the earth, so are my ways higher than your ways and my thoughts than your thoughts" (Isa. 55:9). In other words, he was saying, "I am transcendentally different".

God did not tell the Israelites this in order to intimidate them. His aim was to show them the way that they could become holy, at least on the human level. Earlier in the same passage, Isaiah had written, "Let the wicked forsake their ways and the unrighteous their thoughts. Let

---

[3] R. C. Sproul, *The Holiness of God* (Illinois: Tyndale House, 1985), 54–55.

them turn to the Lord, and he will have mercy on them, and to our God, for he will freely pardon" (Isa. 55:7).

There is a key word in that passage that wipes out the record of past sin that we have been struggling with in this chapter and that gives us a new lease of life. In chapter 2 we saw that our salvation depends on our turning back to God, yet that is not what qualifies us as holy. Nor is forsaking our evil ways the ticket we are looking for. Both of these are important for coming to God at all. But the only thing that will make us holy is God's **pardon**, that is the word we have been looking for! It is forgiveness that makes us holy. Anyone who has been pardoned by God is counted righteous and accepted by God. He or she is therefore different from everyone else!

In Paul's teaching on the subject of holiness, he quotes the psalmist: "Blessed are they whose transgressions are forgiven, whose sins are covered. Blessed are those whose sin the Lord will never count against them" (Rom. 4:7–8). They are not blessed because they sinned, nor because God has licensed them to sin. Never! They are blessed because they are forgiven. They have become children of God, joint heirs to the kingdom of God.

And now I can heave a sigh of relief, we have found the sure way to be admitted to holiness!

This forgiveness is not an arbitrary act, in which God simply decides to make everyone who turns to him holy. No. There is a penalty for sin, a price to be paid – but God paid the full price himself! He satisfied the terms of justice and secured the right to free sinners who trust in his name. Scripture says that, "without the shedding of blood there is no forgiveness", but the passage continues, "so Christ was sacrificed once to take away the sins of many" (Heb. 9:22, 28). On the basis of his sacrifice and the shedding of his blood, the Scripture says, "to all who did receive him, to those who believed in his name, he gave the right to become children of God" (John 1:12). What the Bible is saying is, "because of his sacrifice of himself, Christ separates all who receive him, who believe in his name, and makes them acceptable to God – the children of God!" I could make that last statement at least one more time, and here is it: "Having paid the price for sin, all who receive him, who believe in his name he hallows to make them different from others – children of God". If I were to replace "hallows" in the last statement with "sanctifies", and replace "different from others" with "holy", I would have made the same statement still one more time. Try it for yourself.

This truth is cardinal for any Christian who wants to correctly understand the doctrine of Christ. The writer to the Hebrews said, "And by that will, we have been made holy through the sacrifice of the body of Jesus Christ once for all" (Heb. 10:10). Now check that statement against your rephrasing of John 1:12 in the last paragraph, which should read, "Having paid the price for sin, all who receive him, who believe in his name he sanctifies to become holy, children of God". Our hold on this avenue of pardon as the correct way to become holy is all the more strengthened. Jesus' body was sacrificed once for all, and we who trust in him have been made holy once and for all!

Those who doubt whether forgiveness alone is enough to make us holy should read again the words of the psalmist, "Blessed are those whose transgressions are forgiven, whose sins are covered. Blessed are those whose sin the Lord does not count against them and in whose spirit is no deceit" (Ps. 32:1–2). He is saying that the one blessed above others is the one whose sins are forgiven and covered – that deals with previous sins. At the same time the person's sins are no longer counted against him – that deals with present sins. The psalmist does not tell us how the person got to be in that fortunate position. He must have been led by the Spirit of Christ to anticipate what was to come, although he did not experience it for himself, at least to the fullest extent. This may be why Jesus claimed, "many prophets and righteous people longed to see what you see but did not see it" (Matt. 13:17).

The psalmist also tells us one more thing: God has not arbitrarily exercised his divine authority. The one pardoned has followed the path of belief and repentance, and is free from deceit. The person has been rescued from wilful sin and has turned to God. So we get the picture – the person had sinned, but he or she turned to God. Their sins are forgiven; the records are wiped clear. They have been rescued from deceit. All their dealings before God are now in truth. Even if they still falter at times, their sins are no longer counted against them because heaven reckons them as true: truly anti-sin; truly pro-God, truly pro-righteousness. What one word do you suggest describes the state of such a person? I will not let you beat me to this one; the word is

redeemed. He or she has been freely pardoned and rescued from the deceit of sin. They are saved. They are no longer counted as unrighteous but as righteous, not because they have become invulnerable to sin, but because of an act of God. In other words, they have been justified, and because there is no longer deceit in their spirit, even though they may still sometimes fall, they are in the process of being made more and more holy.

Holiness is not something we achieve; it is something into which we are redeemed. Its foundation is our pardon because of the blood Jesus shed on the cross. Our human holiness can only be maintained because of the same forgiveness. It is only when we exclude God's forgiveness from our ideas of holiness that we are tempted to quit. The Galatian church made the same mistake as we do in thinking that we can add human achievement to our qualifications for justification. Paul saw the inherent danger in such thinking and warned them against it (Gal. 3–5).

We therefore see that we get to be holy by the mercy of God. We are to continue being holy by trusting the mercy of God. If we slip into thinking that we have been justified because of the faith we have achieved, we will run into problems because we will despair as we search for holiness in our further achievements. We were justified because of God's mercy, and so are reckoned as holy. So also his mercy will maintain us in our struggles. Even if we fail at some point or another, his mercy will lift us, sustain us, pardon and strengthen us to continue. Our struggle against the world and sin is what marks us as holy, not our winning every single battle. It is in trusting in the mercy of God that we may grow in holiness.

A Victorious Christian Life

You may still be asking: "How can I live a holy life, being holy in my thoughts, words, deeds, conduct and disposition?" Your desire is to find out how to live victoriously moment by moment. Is this even possible? Yes, there is indeed such a thing as living a holy life. It entails obedience to God through Jesus Christ and results in victory over the flesh, Satan and the world. So when then we talk of holiness, we are talking of a real victory.

But three fundamental problems emerge when we approach holiness solely in terms of victorious Christian living and overcoming opposition.

- **We limit the scope of holiness.** When we define complete holiness as overcoming sin in the sense of gaining victory over negative thoughts, words, deeds and dispositions, we limit the scope of holy living. The all-encompassing view of holiness involves living in obedience to God and in fruitful labour for a lost world.

- **We may encounter potent psychological problems.** This is especially true of those who are just starting to think about holiness or who have strong relationships with others who are outside of Christ. Aiming at victory presents us with the challenge of overcoming an enemy. Some Christians may be so scared by this that they may never even start to think about the real issues involved in holiness. For instance, a youngster who sees holiness as involving confrontation with long-standing friends or respected relations may shrink from pursuing it for fear of the trouble it will arouse.

- **We may use failure as an excuse to abdicate our responsibility.** If we think of holiness in terms of victory, then every failure to achieve holiness is a defeat. It then becomes easy to blame our failure on an external enemy, rather than on our own lack of obedience. We see the same pattern in students who fail examinations and blame the examining bodies, saying, "they did not favour me", instead of stating the truth, "I failed the examination". So we also blame something outside of us, claiming we were overcome, instead of facing up to the truth that "I disobeyed God".

> It might be well if we stopped using the terms "victory" and "defeat" to describe our progress in holiness. Rather we should use the terms "obedience" and "disobedience". When I say I am defeated by some sin, I am unconsciously slipping out from under my responsibility. I am saying something outside of me has defeated me. But when I say I am disobedient, that places the responsibility for my sin squarely on me. We may, in fact, be defeated, but the reason we are defeated is that we have chosen

to disobey. We have chosen to entertain lustful thoughts, or to harbour resentment, or to shade the truth a little.[4]

Once we begin blaming others for our failures, we have reasons to keep failing and may never take any serious steps to stop failing because we are convinced that something external which we cannot control may still overcome us.

It would be better if we took a more comprehensive approach to holiness. Instead of thinking of it in terms of overcoming opposition, we should think of it as pleasing a friend, and a friend who will help us please him. Holiness comes down to wanting to please Jesus more than anyone else. With this perspective, the youngster does not have to focus on holiness as primarily involving confrontation with parents and old friends (in fact, confrontation may not even be necessary).

Think of computer users, especially new ones, and how excited they get while working away at a task that could be exhausting. Some become so involved in what they are doing that they miss meals. The reason they do this is simple. The computer keeps them excited as they explore more and more of its secrets, which it reveals to those who search and search for them. It keeps them working at difficult jobs far longer than they would otherwise do. In the same way, Jesus can be said to be "user-friendly". He has a way of helping those who work at holiness through him, those who through waiting on him and hearing from him seek to obey him by truly living holy lives.

We should view holiness and obedience to God from the perspective of our relationship with Christ, and from the perspective that we are being built up in Christ as we take in more and more of him. This approach will lead to our overcoming the flesh, self, sin and the world, but it will not be done by direct confrontation (even though we will still encounter opposition while obeying). Our own capacity will be replaced by the capacity of the Holy Spirit, and our own talents, strengths, emotions and frailties will be modulated, amplified, moderated or redirected by the indwelling Spirit. This is what Paul meant when he talked of "Christ [being] formed in" the Galatians (Gal. 4:19). A Christian may get so excited about Jesus, so involved with him, that he or she lives in Jesus'

---

[4] Jerry Bridges, *The Pursuit of Holiness* (Singapore: NavPress, 1978), 84.

presence, and in living with Jesus lives for him, and in living for him obeys him, and in obeying him lives a holy life.

This approach to holy living is discussed in more detail in chapter 10. Here we only point out that while "the law" which condemned our sin "came through Moses", "grace and truth", which point out our sin but also help us into true holiness, "came through Jesus Christ" (John 1:16–17). The way into holy living is letting Christ be formed in us. It is this that will challenge us to labour for a lost world and also empower us to keep working and to stand up and be counted for Christ. This is holiness and daily victorious living.

Questions

1. What is the common view of holiness?
2. How can one become truly holy?
3. What price was paid to make us holy?
4. What role does forgiveness play before and after one has become a Christian?
5. What important thing do Christians often make a mistake about in their quest to remain holy?
6. What is the best approach to living a holy life?

4

THE WILDERNESS OF CONFLICTS

Part of what overwhelms victims of inner conflicts is the assumption that they are the only ones who are suffering like this. It is thus worth taking time to reflect on what a normal Christian life looks like. It is a wilderness experience like that of the children of Israel. The story of their redemption from slavery in Egypt offers many parallels to our redemption in Christ Jesus.

A Parallel and a Threshold

We tend to think of the enslavement of Israel in Egypt as political, economic and possibly social, but throughout his campaign for the freedom of the Israelites Moses categorized it under one heading: spiritual enslavement. God continually told Pharaoh through Moses: "Let my people go so that they may worship me" (Exod. 7:16; 8:1; 8:20; etc.). Regardless of how antagonistic Pharaoh was to the Jews, they must still have maintained some kind of worship of God, even if only in the silent recesses of their hearts. But Moses' demand makes it clear that their stay in Egypt impeded their worship of God.

Moses' request to Pharaoh parallels the reason for our own redemption: we are called to worship the Lord "in the Spirit and in truth" (John 4:23). Both redemption stories stem from the need to go and serve the Lord. We tend to think that the Israelites were being called to go and possess the land of milk and honey and escape their servitude. But the milk and honey were consequent upon their serving the Lord. Even if

Israel did worship quietly in Egypt, they needed to embrace unfettered worship of God. Only then would they blossom in the full providence of God's blessings. The same is true of our worship of God. Some of us may have worshipped half-heartedly and not enjoyed unhindered communion with God. But now through Christ we can be redeemed so that we worship in spirit and truth, not as aliens but as children.

The apostles recognized the parallels and continuity between these two redemption stories. For example, in introducing the gospel of Jesus Christ to his largely Gentile readers, John found it convenient to point to the summit of the covenant of Moses as being only the threshold of the covenant of Jesus Christ. He wanted them to realize that the redemption through Moses was similar to, but fell far short of, the redemption by Jesus. Thus he wrote, "Out of his [Jesus'] fullness we have all received grace in place of grace already given. For the law was given through Moses; grace and truth came through Jesus Christ" (John 1:16–17). In contrasting the two redemptions, John did not see them as opposites. He saw the former as a type, a foreshadowing, that was of a lower order than the latter as well as a step towards it. How do we know this? In the same context, John wrote of the blessings we receive from Jesus' grace as things we could never receive from Moses' law. The author of Hebrews knew the same thing when he wrote: "The law is only a shadow of the good things that are coming" (Heb. 10:1).

The law marked the summit of the covenant of Moses. All who were part of that covenant lived under the law. Their relationship with God was inevitably a master–slave relationship. Paul explains:

> As long as heirs are underage they are no different from slaves, although they own the whole estate. They are subject to guardians and trustees until the time set by their fathers. So also, when we were underage, we were in slavery under the elemental spiritual forces of the world. But when the set time had fully come, God sent his Son, born of a woman, born under the law, to redeem those under law, that we might receive adoption to sonship (Gal. 4:1–5).

When the law ruled, the relationship was a law relationship, a master–slave relationship; but when grace came through Jesus Christ, we were redeemed from the law to walk fully with God as sons. Our grace relationship is a father–son affair. Slaves live in fear of punishment if they break a single one of their master's rules; a mature son lives in the freedom of his father's love.

The laws set for slaves are intended to control them and prevent them from approaching the master too closely or knowing him too well. They maintain a distance, just as God did at Mount Sinai when he told Moses: "Put limits for the people around the mountain" (Exod. 19:12). But in family relationships, the son and the father work hard to be together, and the father is delighted to be with his son. In the same way, we are now invited to, "draw near to God with a sincere heart in full assurance of faith" (Heb. 10:22).

It was not unknown for a slave to move from a position of subservience to a position of trust. Joseph, for example, enjoyed favour in the house of Pharaoh (Gen. 41:39–45). Moses was transmuted from an Israelite slave boy to a member of Pharaoh's family (Exod. 2:1–10). Daniel received great favour in the kingdom of Nebuchadnezzar (Dan. 2). This is the hope that the Apostle John is holding out to us with his upbeat introduction in John 1:16–17. He wants us to realize that through Jesus we can now move beyond the law-covenant and enter a higher level of interpersonal relationship with God, a relationship in which we "are no longer foreigners and strangers, but ... members of [God's] household" (Eph. 2:19).

Our strongest justification for seeing parallels between the Old and the New Testaments is our Lord Jesus himself, who

> affirmed that Abraham had rejoiced to see his day, that Moses had written of him, that the Scriptures bore witness to him, and that indeed in the three great divisions of the Old Testament – the law, the prophets and the writings – there were 'things concerning himself.' [1]

So accepting this redemption story of Israel as truly foreshadowing and pointing to our redemption in Christ Jesus, we will try to use this story to shed light on the new covenant in Christ Jesus.

---

[1] R. W. Stott, *Basic Christianity* (Illinois: InterVarsity Press, 1971), 23–24.

The first thing you should notice is something about the book of Exodus itself. It opens with a brief description of the Israelites' entry into Egypt and the prosperity that led them to stay there, but quickly moves on to describe the oppression they later began to endure. Then from chapter 2 to chapter 12 verse 30, it records evangelistic efforts as God reaches out to deliver his people from slavery. The section from verse 31 of chapter 12 through chapter 14 records the actual deliverance from Egypt. But after this, the rest of the book of Exodus, and the entire books of Leviticus, Numbers, Deuteronomy and Joshua, all record what is commonly referred to as Israel's journey in the wilderness; the journey which should have taken them forty days but which unfortunately spanned forty years. It was a very tedious journey, very risky, full of trials, temptations, turmoil, costly wars, sweet victories, costly failures, judgements and great acts of faith in walking with God.

There is a reason why so much space is given to recording the details of this wilderness journey. The writer of 1 Corinthians says it was recorded to serve as a map for those of us who would be part of the later wilderness experience (1 Cor. 10:1–11).

A Map of the Wilderness

Maps are invaluable sources of information. We refer to them when we have to drive through unknown neighbourhoods. Wildlife biologists use them to record where particular animals are and in what quantities. Engineers use survey maps to help them plot the routes for railways and roads. Sailors use nautical maps, or charts, to navigate from one harbour to the next.

Imagine what it would be like if administrators had to tour dozens of towns each time they had to make any decisions that required information about the population, telephone lines, electricity supply, pipelines, markets and roads. They would soon be exhausted! A map makes it all easy. The officials can sit in their offices and tour the entire state, stopping to focus on the exact points that are of interest. They can measure the size of farms, determine what crops are grown and the volume of production. They can find out what types of animal life are present and so can adhere to and enforce wildlife policies. The map can even contribute to ingenious decisions about erosion control policies as the officials identify the forces that are causing erosion. Police and security officials refer to maps as they fight crime and plan military operations. We owe a great debt of gratitude to the surveyors who make these maps for us.

A survey map can be especially useful when one is trying to find one's way through a forest in which there are few roads or through an uninhabited wilderness. Moses would probably have appreciated a map as he led the Israelites out of Egypt, although it is us unlikely that he had one.

Here, however, I will try to give you a map of the New Testament wilderness experience. My map will show you the length of the journey, the dangerous wildlife you will encounter, the forces at play and the scope of the entire battle you are caught up in. Studying the map will show you that there is only one path that leads through the wilderness – persevering faith.

There has always been less confusion about what we are saved from than about the process of our redemption. We all agree that we are saved from sin and from the wrath of God. We also agree that it is by the blood of Jesus, that is, by his sacrificial death, that we are redeemed. But we agree less about how he who redeems us transports us from the state where we "have sinned and fall short of the glory of God" (Rom. 3:23), to the state of being "without stain or wrinkle or any other blemish, but holy and blameless" (Eph. 5:27). The questions that we disagree on are these: Are we saved to perfection here and now? If not, how do we remain in a relationship with God while we are not yet absolutely perfect? When are we to be perfected, and through what process? It is these questions I hope to answer by looking at that Exodus redemption story in the Old Testament.

Our redemption starts with our being reconciled to God, or to use a more technical word, at the point of our justification. That is the point at which God accepts us back as his own children. The reason for this acceptance is, first, the death of Jesus Christ on the cross as a sacrifice atoning for our previous defiance and insubordination to God, and, secondly, our affirmation of faith in Christ Jesus as our Saviour from sin and our submission to God's sovereignty and supremacy. We acknowledge our dependence on God and renounce self and its selfish inclinations.

While justification starts our redemption, the end to which redemption is to bring us is glorification, the place where we are perfectly united with God in will and enraptured by his glory, perfectly satisfied to worship him all day. When we reach that state, sin will never, even for a split second, come between us and God; we shall never be tempted, but will blossom in the light of his glory, imperishable and perfected in glory and power.

Justification is the point at which God "rescued us from the dominion of darkness and brought us into the kingdom of the Son he loves" (Col. 1:13). It is the point where we cross the borders of enslavement to self and sin. The Old Testament parallel is the day after the first Passover, when the Israelites stepped out of Egypt. That was the point at which God delivered them from the shackles of slavery that had deprived them of any hope and any meaningful experience of God and brought them under the canopy of his own presence as symbolized by the pillars of fire and of cloud.

Our justification anticipates the promised land of our glorification, where our freedom and perfection in Christ will be fully consummated, where "we will be with the Lord forever" (1 Thess. 4:17). The Exodus also anticipated the land of Canaan, the land promised to Abraham, Isaac and Jacob as a possession where their children would enjoy limitless opportunities and prosperity as they freely worshipped Yahweh, the God of their fathers.

Between the escape from Egypt and the entry into Canaan, however, was a wilderness experience that should have lasted forty days, but unfortunately lasted forty years. In our own redemption in Christ, do we recognize any such space between the moment we are rescued from slavery into the freedom of sons of God and the moment when we are admitted into the incorruptible perfect glory of the very presence of God? The answer must be yes. There is a parallel wilderness experience for us, for we did not step out of bondage of sin straight into the perfect glory of heaven.

It will help us to grasp the extent of this wilderness and the path through it, if we identify some distinguishing features of the border lands surrounding the wilderness. We will thus look forward to our future in glory and back to our bondage to sin in the past.

Are We There Yet?

Paul gives us a strong clue to what we shall be like in glory: "So will it be with the resurrection of the dead. The body that is sown is perishable, it is raised imperishable; it is sown in dishonour, it is raised in glory, it is sown in weakness, it is raised in power; it is sown a natural body, it is raised a spiritual body" (1 Cor. 15:42–44). Thus we can safely say that when we reach our destination we will be:

- **Immortal:** In heaven we will never die. Sickness is a mark of mortality. Anything that gets sick may die. When we become immortal, we will never be sick.

- **Glorious:** While we are on earth, we are defiled and have "spots and wrinkles". In heaven we will have no trace of defilement physically, morally or spiritually. We will be sinless. Just as sickness is an indicator of mortality, so vulnerability to temptation is a pointer to sinfulness. Anyone who can be tempted can fall into sin.

- **Powerful:** In heaven we shall be clothed with the power to do all that we want to do. Our inability to do the things we want to do is one of the frustrations we live with on this side of eternity.

- **Spiritual:** The body we will be clothed with in heaven is a spiritual body. We can get some understanding of what a spiritual body is if we think about Jesus' body after his resurrection. It was tangible, but it had the ability to be anywhere at any instant without travelling through time and space. It could enter a locked room without hindrance. Jesus also said that our resurrected bodies will be like those of angels, in that we will neither "marry nor be given in marriage" (Matt. 22:30). So it may be that in heaven we will be neuter, rather than men or women.

These qualities of a glorified person must occur together: we cannot have one of them without having all the others. They are all linked. So, for example, we cannot hope to become entirely sinless while still remaining vulnerable to death.

We certainly do not see these glorified qualities in our lives now. We are not sinless and are certainly not free of the attention of the evil one. Nor can we claim that all our needs are met; we still suffer lack. Sometimes we are tired or sick, and we will die unless the Lord returns first. We have not yet started doing everything we want to do, nor stopped doing all the things we don't want to do. In fact, as Paul says, "We ourselves … groan inwardly as we wait eagerly for our adoption, the redemption of our bodies" (Rom. 8:23). Clearly we are not yet glorified!

Does saying that we have not yet been glorified, mean that we are not yet saved? No! We will be greatly helped by looking at that profound statement by the beloved apostle: "Dear friends, now we are children of God, and what we will be has not yet been made known. But we know that when Christ appears, we shall be like him, for we shall see him as he is" (1 John 3:2). Yes, right now we are children of God; we are saved already. But what we will be cannot yet be described, partly because we have not yet become what we will be, and partly because what we will be is incomprehensible to us as we are now.

Some may claim that the fact that we have not yet attained these qualities shows we are not yet saved from sin. To answer them, we need to go back and look at what we used to be before the Son of God started reforming us from within.

Are We Still There?

What were we like when we were without Christ?

- **Egocentric:** Before we were saved, we were dead in sin (Eph. 2:1). The heartbeat of sin is selfishness, and everything we did was motivated primarily by selfish considerations. The most important person to be considered in anything I did was me. Some of us were strong in doing evil to protect, promote and gratify ourselves. Others of us were weak in doing good in an attempt to secure and preserve better positions for ourselves. The king of my life was me, and if it was necessary to defy or at least ignore God's word in order to achieve my purpose, so be it. We thought of God as remote, and our self-interest blocked any sensitivity to him. Sometimes we even doubted there was a God. At other times we declared that there was no God (even if we did not dare say this aloud, our actions showed that it was what we believed). We thought of God as little more than a remote figment of our imagination. He was a stranger, an unwelcome stranger, and any serious thought about him made us utterly uncomfortable. We did not trust him to provide for our needs but relied on our own resources. We may have prayed for things, but that was only a formality. We did not really care who answered our prayers. We would have been happy to have our needs met even by the devil himself, especially if he appeared well dressed and sophisticated and possibly even mentioned the name of God. We were dead in sin because we were dead to God and alive only to ourselves.

- **Restless:** When we were not yet saved, we were without faith, assured of nothing. An unbelieving man is worried because he needs to make money; when he gets money, he is worried that thieves may take it from him. He is worried because he wants to marry a beautiful wife; when he succeeds, he fears that his wife's beauty will cause her to be unfaithful. He suffers from deep inner insecurity because his life is anchored in the shifting sands of self and material things. He is intensely worried and insecure, at the mercy of his fiery imagination. This uncertainty of life, of love, and of guaranteed help from the source of all good things plagues both men and women, and may account for the increasing number of drug abusers and alcoholics all over the world. For many, drugs and alcohol deaden the inner rumble of insecurity.

- **Enslaved:** When we were not yet saved, we practised sin, at least so it seemed. But that was only as long as we played along and kept faith with sin. When we chose to quit sin, it revealed its real nature. It was not something we practised; it was something that had mastered us. We were its slaves. We did not have the self-control to quit. For example, a man might decide to stop having extramarital affairs. Everything would go smoothly for the first few days. Then the monster within (the old nature) would rise up and pat him on the back: "Congratulations! You've done it. You've kept away from other women for all this time, and there is no reason you can't keep this up for the rest of your life. But why not take a break? Relax for a bit. Just once more, and then you can stay away from other women for as long as you wish. But why not have just one final fling?" And then the man begins to argue: "Certainly not! But it would do no harm and might relax me if I just drove past the red light corner, just to see my old friends and maybe advise them to quit too. I won't even step out of my car." So he goes. And he is welcomed by his friends, and offered a cigarette, and his determination crumbles. He doesn't want to offend his friends, and so he agrees, "Just this once". His slavery continues.

I have just described some of the things that characterized our lives when we were without Christ. But from the day I denied myself and turned to God, there has been a new king in my life. His will takes precedence. But for some reason, that does not breed insecurity. Rather, I am at peace in a way that passes ordinary understanding. Even if my whole world comes crumbling down on me, I am assured that there is one who is almighty who supports me and takes care of my life. When death stares me straight in the face, I do not become despondent, for my Lord is in charge of life and death. "For to me, to live is Christ and to die is gain" (Phil. 1:21). If God chooses that I die, I am not scared of an unknown destination. I am heading straight into his bosom, where the Scripture says of those who die in Christ, "Never again will they hunger; never again will they thirst. The sun will not beat down on them, nor any scorching heat. For the Lamb at the centre before the throne will be their shepherd; he will lead them to springs of living water. And God will wipe away every tear from their eyes" (Rev. 7:16–17). As for my loved ones, my wife and family, they are in good hands with the same Lord who is good and faithful in all things to those who trust him.

I may not have become perfect in dealing with sin moment by moment, but I am no longer a slave to sin. I no longer seek out sins to commit, nor do I fix my eyes on sin. My eyes are lifted up to the Lord to see how I can please him. My inclination is to do good. If I do wrong, I am deeply distressed. I only find joy if I have pleased God. My tendency is towards righteousness. I love God; I go for God. I hate sin; I flee from it.

I notice that the sinful nature in me still loves the dark fringes of my past and pulls me to visit there from time to time. Yet a stronger force is at work in me, driving me to pursue the silver lining on the horizon ahead. I know that is the right thing to do, but sometimes I despair for the path is rough, the terrain tedious, and the distance overwhelming. Yet despite moments of despair, sin no longer has dominion over me. By God's grace I live a righteous life.

We can say, "I am no longer what I used to be; yet I have not fully become what I am to be". If people focus on the lower nature still struggling in me, they will call me a sinner. If they recognize the work of God in me, and the consistent manner in which righteousness grows in me while sin is shrinking, they can project to what I will ultimately become and call me a saint. But even when I am called a sinner, I am no longer a sinner dead in sin, I am a sinner saved by grace. When I am called a saint, I am not yet a saint glorified, I am a saint being sanctified.

A Luta Continua!

Our study of the boundary territories has made it clear that while we have not yet arrived in our Canaan of perfection in heaven, we no longer dwell in the Egypt of sin. We are somewhere between the two. Here on earth, we are living our wilderness experience. But why? What is the key purpose of this wilderness experience?

For the Israelites, the time in the wilderness was a time when the Lord tested the faith of those he had rescued from Egypt. Did they really believe? Would they really obey him? It was also a period of training for those who did really believe. They were disciplined and humbled and shown what it means to "live on every word that comes from the mouth of the Lord". It was also a period when those who did not really have faith (as shown by their disobedience to God) were dropped from entering the Promised Land (Heb. 3:16–19, Deut. 8:2–5). It is instructive that the last grumblings among the Israelites came towards the end of the wilderness journey, just about when Moses handed over to Joshua. Those who remained were disciplined enough to trust in God and confront the Anakites (Deut. 9:2).

An earlier redemption story in Genesis 19 also illustrates the wilderness experience. In that story, the focus of redemption was Lot (Gen. 19:12). His family could join him in escaping judgement, but the condition for escaping was faith. Did they believe that God was going to judge sin? Did they now see sin as despicable? If they did, they should flee from sin without turning back. Lot's wife, an example of those who did not quite believe, turned to face the land of sin, and became a mound of salt. She missed the Promised Land.

One more lesson we can learn from Lot is that the wilderness experience calls for perseverance (Heb. 12:1). There will still be strong forces working to pull us back. Our only hope of surviving is to keep focused on God and our destination. This is what the author of Hebrews encourages us to do, when he says, "Let us fix our eyes on Jesus, the pioneer and perfecter of faith" (Heb. 12:2). Only those who come in by faith will persevere. Those who do not have the "wedding garment" of faith will become worn out and drop by the wayside.

These stories underline the key truth variously expressed in the Bible but hardly believed by most of us: our salvation here on earth does not destroy our sinful nature or our humanity. What it does do is to awaken each one's spirit from its life-long lethargy and through the Holy Spirit empower the human spirit to engage the weakened flesh so as to constantly rule and make righteousness reign in our mortal bodies.

As for the sinful nature, it is the stumbling block that trips up those without faith. But those who are truly born of God will eventually step over this stumbling block, "for everyone born of God overcomes the world. This is the victory that has overcome the world, even our faith" (1 John 5:4).

The cry *A luta continua!* is common among pressure groups in Nigeria. I learned it when I was a student. Each time we staged a demonstration to compel the school authorities to look into our welfare, there would be shouts of, "A luta continua! A luta continua!! A luta continua!!!" I used to think it was a proclamation of victory because in those first encounters we got what we demanded. I was later to learn what "a luta" really means. As someone graciously explained: "Whether we win or lose a struggle with the authorities, the struggle for students' welfare never ends till we are out of school. A luta continua – the struggle continues!"

When I use the same saying with regard to Christians' struggle, I am not implying that we are engaged in a power struggle between equals, as though our old and new selves were engaged in a continuous wrestling match to see which will overpower the other. At some stages of the Christian life, that may appear to be the case, but there is really no contest. The new self, filled with the Holy Spirit, will defeat the old. The flesh will always seek to influence our decisions, but the shout of faith is

"A luta continua!" The sinful nature is here to struggle with us, and the sooner we acknowledge this truth the better. If we fail to acknowledge it, we are caught at a disadvantage when the flesh spring surprises on us. Forewarned is forearmed!

It is now time to turn to see what God expects our lives to be like here on earth now that we know it is he who allows us to endure this struggle with our inherently sinful nature.

Clash of the Titans

Paul told the Christians at Colossae: "Put to death, therefore, whatever belongs to your earthly nature: sexual immorality, impurity, lust, evil desires and greed, which is idolatry" (Col. 3:5). We are to mortify these deeds of the sinful nature now that each of us has "put on the new self, which is being renewed in knowledge in the image of its Creator" (Col. 3:10). Through our own wilderness experience, we are being transformed and are developing Christ-like characters, but we still need to put to death the deeds of our sinful nature in order for our spiritual transformation to progress.

We must take it upon ourselves to fight the sinful nature in its dual personification in the flesh and self. The sinful nature will not give in easily. It grew very strong over the years when we fed it with sin, and it still has many resources in our ignorance of life, as well as reserves in our memory of the wrong we have known and once admired. It is quite ruthless and can easily pull some straggling cords in what we read, hear or see in a sinning world. Nevertheless, we have an advantage: we are in control, not that sinful nature. No matter how much it pulls us to do something, we can say no. With time as we exclusively feed and exercise our spirits in righteousness through studying and meditating on God's word, prayer and obedience to God, the flesh will become starved and its strength depleted. Above all, the Holy Spirit supplies us with enormous strength that, rightly applied, will overwhelm the sinful nature.

Paul also taught the Galatians: "Those who sow to their sinful nature, from that nature will reap destruction; those who sow to please the Spirit, from the Spirit will reap eternal life" (Gal. 6:8). Sow to the Spirit, pander to the Spirit, deny the flesh, starve the sinful nature: that is how to fight the good fight. Just as the righteous nature went comatose when we gave in to sinning, if we remain in the will of God, learning new things through our obedience to God, the flesh will also be moribund. Take one battle at a time. Do not ever be overwhelmed when the flesh bothers you about how much longer you will need to keep fighting. Take each battle as it comes; do not worry about tomorrow's battles.

You need to know what these struggles are all about. In the past, the devil's aim was to stop you from ever coming to salvation in Christ Jesus. Now that you have come to Christ, his plan is to attack your faith through the flesh, so that you quit. If he gets you to sin, he will heap blame on you and suggest you quit, either by convincing you that the faith does not work or that God will not accept you any longer because you have sinned.

The truth is that the real victory has been won for you at the cross of Christ. Jesus said, "In this world you will have trouble. But take heart! I have overcome the world" (John 16:33). "Do not be afraid, little flock, for your Father has been pleased to give you the kingdom" (Luke 12:32). Do not ever quit, nor give in to sin because that will wean your heart from God, making you take him for granted. Remain hooked to the Spirit; keep true to your faith.

The Dialectics of Sin

The presence of the sinful nature within me and the call on me to overcome it are important issues in my relationship with God. He knows that the sinful nature, which draws me to sin, is within me and he accepts me as his own just the way I am. He knows that my sinful nature leaves me vulnerable to sin, but he counts me righteous because of my faith in the Lord Jesus Christ. As I look back, I see that I have been saved from sin; but I look forward to see that I have not yet been caught up into perfect glory. What I am called to is a life of vigorous pursuit of a very high calling but lower attainment – yet an attainment that is too high to be regarded as still wallowing in the lowly places of sinfulness.

Some notable theologians have written about this wilderness experience. This is what John Stott has to say about it:

> Already God has put his Holy Spirit within us, in order to make us holy (1 Thess. 4:7–8). Already the Spirit is actively at

work within us, subduing our fallen, selfish human nature and causing his ninefold fruit to ripen in our character (Gal. 5:16–26). Already, we can affirm, he is transforming us by degrees into the image of Christ (2 Cor. 3:18).

Not yet, however, has our fallen nature been eradicated, for still "the sinful nature desires what is contrary to the Spirit" (Gal. 5:17), so that "if we claim to be without sin, we deceive ourselves" (1 John 1:8). Not yet have we become completely conformed to God's perfect will, for not yet do we love God with all our being, or our neighbour as ourselves. These things await the coming of Christ. As Paul put it, we have "not ... already been made perfect", but we "press on towards the goal", confident that "he who began a good work in [us] will carry it on to completion until the day of Christ Jesus" (Phil. 3:12–14; 1:6).

So then, we are caught in a painful dialectic between the "now" and the "not yet", between defeat and victory, between dismay over our continuing failures and the promise of ultimate freedom, between the cry of longing, "Who will rescue me from this body of death?" and the cry of assurance, "Thanks be to God – through Jesus Christ our Lord!" (Rom. 7:24–25). On the one hand, we must take with the utmost seriousness God's command, "Be holy because I ... am holy" (e.g. Lev. 19:2), Jesus' instruction, "Go, and do not sin again" (John 8:11), and John's statements that he is writing so that his readers "will not sin", and that "no-one who is born of God will continue to sin" (1 John 2:1; 3:9). On the other hand, we have to acknowledge the reality of indwelling sin alongside the reality of the indwelling Spirit (e.g. Rom. 7:17, 20; 8:9, 11). The sinless perfection we long for continues to elude us, although in rejecting perfectionism, we refuse to embrace reductionism, that is, to acquiesce in low standards of attainment.[2]

The American theologian, R. C. Sproul puts it like this:

---

[2] John R. W. Stott, *The Contemporary Christian* (Leicester: InterVarsity Press, 1992), 385–386.

Teachers argue that there is healing in the atonement of Christ. Indeed there is. Jesus bore all of our sins upon the cross. Yet none of us is free of sin in this life. None of us is free of sickness in this life. The healing that is in the cross is real. We participate in its benefits now, in this life. But the fullness of the healing of both sin and disease takes place in heaven. We still must die when it is our appointed time.[3]

Dr. Stott offers us more insight by quoting Bishop Handley Moule. Speaking about the aims of Christians, Moule wrote:

> We aim at nothing less than to walk with God all day long; to abide every hour in Christ...; to love God with all the heart and our neighbour as ourselves...; to "yield ourselves to God"...; to break with all evil, and follow all good ... We are absolutely bound to put quite aside all secret purposes of moral compromise, all tolerance of besetting sin... We cannot possibly rest short of a daily, hourly, continuous walk with God, in Christ, by the grace of the Holy Ghost.[4]

But Moule also spoke of the limits to what we can achieve:

> I hold with absolute conviction, alike from the experience of the church and from the infallible Word, that, in the mystery of things, there will be limits to the last, and very humbling limits, very real fallings short. To the last it will be a *sinner* that walks with God.[5]

We need to remember the words of John Newton, the converted slave-trader, who is reputed to have said: "I am not what I ought to be, I am not what I want to be, I am not what I hope to be in another world, but still I am not what I once used to be, and by the grace of God I am what I am".[6]

---

[3] R. C. Sproul, *Surprised by Suffering* (Illinois: Tyndale House, 1988), 19.
[4] H. C. G. Moule, *Thoughts on Christian Sanctity* (London: Seeley, 1888), as quoted in Stott, *The Contemporary Christian* (Leicester: InterVarsity Press, 1992), 385–386.
[5] Ibid.
[6] J. C. Ryle, *Home Truths* (London: Charles Thynne, n.d.), as quoted in John R. W. Stott, *The Contemporary Christian*, 386.

If we look again at one of Paul's insights he wrote; "And just as we have borne the image of the earthly man, so shall we bear the image of the heavenly man" (1 Cor. 15:49). Till the Lord takes us to be with him forever, we are bound to the fate of bearing the likeness of the earthly man – his frailties and limitations – while striving to conform to our calling to be like the man from heaven.

While we have been saved from sin, God does not guarantee that the wants and needs through which desire gives birth to temptation are extinguished here. God expects the believer to remain obedient despite those desires, learning obedience and the futility of sinful passions and fancies. It is for this reason that the Holy Spirit is given to live in us, so that he will supply us with his strength to match our weakness until Jesus comes to perfect us and it becomes natural for us to be spiritual. Then having been redeemed from all earthly dross and contamination and transformed into glory without lack or deformity, we shall fully reflect the image of the one who created us in his own image.

In our wilderness experience, we sometimes keep quiet when we should have spoken out. Sometimes, we have punished when we should have listened in compassion. At other times we have felt some tinge of secret delight when we should have shared the pains of God over sin and human lostness. We have often looked the other way while someone else suffered injustice or misfortune. Sometimes we have played Jonah, hoping that God will destroy the wicked "Ninevite" sinners rather than caring that they are lost. Or we have joined the young Apostle John in picking arguments with those who do not agree with us or attend our own church (Mark 9:38). We may also have thought ourselves superior, like the Jews, and distanced ourselves from ordinary Samaritans, that is, the sinners we make out to be the incurable scum of the earth, in order to retain our positions with God. It is quite true that "if we say we have no sin we deceive ourselves" (1 John 1:8).

Each time we become conscious of our sins, we should mourn over them, confessing them to our Father. But then we should stop, pick ourselves up and again head for the attainment of our high calling. God knows we suffer these shortcomings, but he expects us not to give in to sin, nor to quit the race just because we failed at one point. Our Father in heaven bids us run on towards our high calling.

The real bedrock of these problems of our life on earth is that we only "know in part" (1 Cor. 13:12). If we knew as God knows, if we understood the causes and effects of injustice, hatred, pride, pain and sin in their full details and also knew the benefits of love, mercy and righteousness, and how to attain them, we would share the same pain that God feels over sin, and share in his joy in righteousness. Then we would be different: we would be perfect. For God's "people are destroyed from lack of knowledge" (Hos. 4:6). So we join the Apostle Paul in hoping that, "when perfection comes ... I shall know fully" (1 Cor. 13:10–12 KJV).

In this world we are often tempted, we may some times fall, but that fall does not kill our relationship with God. If we sincerely trust him to help us out of sin, then we improve by the day and enjoy him better. We must get up if we fall and press on towards the mark.

Questions

1. What does the author call the experience we are having now, between our justification and our glorification?
2. What are the features of our wilderness experience?
3. What use does it have?
4. How can we overcome in our wilderness experience?

5

THE SECURITY OF OUR SALVATION

The fact that we experience inner conflicts and the temptation to fall away from the faith raises another vital question: How secure is our salvation? Are there equal chances of a believer falling away from or persevering to ultimate redemption, or is there an external superforce that will keep the believer secure for ultimate redemption?

Our answer to this question depends on our understanding of two important concepts, justification and sanctification.

Justification

If you were to meet the reformer Martin Luther, or the Apostle Paul for that matter, in a twenty-first century theological college and ask them the rich young man's question of Matthew chapter 19, "What good thing must I do to get eternal life?", you would expect them to maintain the Master's position that there is nothing in the world you can do to get eternal life. But if you were a good theology student (and thus apt in juggling words), you would quickly rephrase your question, "How may I inherit eternal life?" At least one of them would probably answer, "By justification". Then there would be a long pause as he looked in your bewildered face to be sure that what he had said sank in.

What does "justification" mean? The Apostle Paul explained it like this to the Christians in Rome, "Righteousness is given through faith in Jesus Christ to all who believe. There is no difference between Jew and Gentile, for all have sinned and fall short of the glory of God, and all are justified freely by his grace through the redemption that came by Christ Jesus" (Rom. 3:22–24).

No matter how many good things we do, we can never really be just or righteous on their account because we have all sinned. But God treats believers as just because they believe in Jesus Christ. To put it in formal terms, justification is the act by which God counts a sinner to be righteous because of the sinner's trust in the sacrificial death of our Lord Jesus Christ as availing for his own sin and unrighteousness. The justified person is counted as having completely satisfied all the demands of the law. Thus someone who has been justified is immediately fully qualified for heaven.

When we speak of the justification of sinners rather than their punishment, we are not indulging in wishful thinking. We are speaking on the authoritative basis that "just as through the disobedience of the one man the many were made sinners, so also through the obedience of the one man the many will be made righteous" (Rom. 5:19). Jesus, who "had no sin" was obedient unto death, paying the price of sin so that all who have sinned but who trust in him will be made the "righteousness of God" (2 Cor. 5:21). He paid the full price; the demands of the law were fully met. All that we have to do is believe in "the Lamb of God, that takes away the sin of the world".

Sanctification

We run into a problem, however, if we stop our discussion of our new relationship with God at the point of justification. Justification is instantaneous when we believe – but then we have to carry on living our new lives in Christ. What do we do then?

The answer is that once we come to faith, we enter into a continuous, life-transforming process called sanctification. It is a direct result of our continued trust in and obedience to Jesus Christ to help us with our frailties and struggles. Sanctification is the continuous process by which we are forgiven, enlightened, strengthened, purified, revived, cleansed and refreshed to continue in our walk of faith with Christ Jesus. Everyone who has been justified is also being sanctified, that is, being made pure in character and disposition. Justification itself creates an irrepressible hunger for sanctification. Being restored to fellowship with God leads to a hunger and thirst for being restored to the image of God.

If we see no signs of sanctification, we may doubt whether a person has been justified. The two go together. The situation is the same as when a baby is born. The very first thing that baby must do is take a breath. If it does not start to breathe and continue breathing, it will die. Exactly the same thing happens at spiritual birth. The first breath of spiritual life is the faith that results in justification. But newborn believers have to continue breathing – their faith has to continue to express itself in sanctification. Without faith, their new life will slowly wither away and die.

Eternal Security?

That last sentence must have drawn the ire of some who consider the statement anathema. They hold to the doctrine of eternal security, which teaches that once one is saved (justified), one is forever justified and must be resurrected and glorified on the last day. This doctrine is acceptable as long as its strong link between justification and glorification is matched by an equally strong link between justification and sanctification. Sanctification must be seen as a compulsory consequence of justification.

We need to pay heed to Jesus' words, "those who stand firm to the end will be saved" (Matt. 10:22). Why did he issue such a warning to those he had called to himself? Judas Iscariot, who was one of those warned, was not ultimately saved. He was "the one doomed to destruction" (John 17:12). Why did Paul claim, "I strike a blow to my body and make it my slave so that after I have preached to others, I myself will not be disqualified for the prize" (1 Cor. 9:27)? Why did he shed tears for some members of the Philippian church who lived "as enemies of the cross of Christ? Their destiny is destruction, their god is their stomach, and their glory is in their shame. Their mind is on earthly things" (Phil. 3:18–19). Why would their destiny be destruction and not ultimate redemption? John says it is because, "they went out from us, but they did not really belong to us. For if they had belonged to us, they would have remained with us" (1 John 2:19). Who are these people? Jude speaks of them as "certain individuals whose condemnation was written about long ago [who] have secretly slipped in among you" (Jude 4). And what distinguishes them? "They are ungodly people, who pervert the grace of our God into a licence for immorality ... [they] pollute their own bodies, reject authority and heap abuse on celestial beings" (Jude 4–8). Jude claimed that such behaviour was nothing new. These people were merely following the pattern of some of those the Lord delivered from Egypt but later destroyed because they did not believe. How did they show that they did not believe? By plunging into sin and giving themselves to immorality and disobedience. (You can read more about this in Jude 1–16.) New Testament people who give themselves over to immorality do so for the very same reason – they do not really believe. If they did, they would give themselves to becoming sanctified.

The truth is that our justification must be followed by our sanctification which daily refreshes our relationship and experience with God, thus sustaining our faith. We cannot stagnate; we are either progressing towards God or we are going away from him. The more we progress towards God, the more difficult it will be for the devil to deceive us, draw us back from God, and do us any harm by getting us to sin.

The passages I have cited here do contain traces of the idea of eternal predestination, which is the basis for the doctrine of eternal security. Jude refers to "individuals whose condemnation was written about long ago" (Jude 4); John claims that they only "went out from us [because] they did not really belong to us" (1 John 2:19). He is saying that those who really belong to us, those who are really justified, will never abandon the faith. But such people would not live as enemies of the cross (Phil. 3:18–19), nor change the grace of God into a licence for immorality. So if the apostles taught eternal security, it was not in the form of an absolute, unconditional guarantee. Rather, they taught that those who are eternally predestined for glorification are eternally predestined for justification and eternally predestined for sanctification. These three must be thoroughly and strongly tied together: Glorification is only possible through sanctification-maintained justification.

Life-Long Insecurity?

It is also important to look at the other side of the coin, and consider whether we are condemned to live with life-long insecurity about our salvation. This brings us to a key point of difference between Christianity and Eastern religions – their teaching about meriting glory. Christians maintain that no mortal can ever deserve to achieve glory. It must be accepted as a gift God gives the sinner who turns to him. Eastern religions teach that by meditation and mental and psychic exercises such as yoga and quietism, one can improve one's purity and position oneself for ascent to higher planes of existence. They fail to recognize that all evil is done against a cosmic being, that is, against God. So they simply sweep their sins under the carpet and pretend they never existed. Even the laws which they obey to attain their "purity" are what Paul dismisses as "harsh treatment of the body, but they lack any value in restraining sensual indulgence" (Col. 2:23).

But while Christians disagree with these religions in principle, our actions sometimes suggest otherwise. Some Christians assume that the sanctification process will blossom in ever-increasing righteousness and ever-depleting sinfulness until our sinfulness hits zero and our righteousness clocks infinity, and then God takes us to heaven. We might even be able to find Christians who assume that God keeps us on earth until we manage this. They think that God so designs our lives that just as we hit the mark he whips us away, as finally having qualified for heaven. This may be all they imply when they say such things as "be ready for the coming of the Lord".

We need to recognize that these believers do base their qualification to start the race of redemption on the grace of God expressed in the sacrificial death of the Lord Jesus. They admit that they could never have been born again were it not for his grace. They also do not deny the need for grace to live victoriously each day. We have no quarrel with them on these points. But the bone of contention is that they think that they have to reach a certain level of purity before they qualify for heaven.

And it is here that we say no! Agreed, we are justified by the grace of God. Agreed, we are to live victoriously each day by the grace of God. Agreed even that our level of victory should increase from one day to the next. But there is no level of purity that we can attain on earth that would qualify us for heaven. On the day of ultimate redemption of our souls, grace will still be needed. From the day we are justified on earth, to the day we are redeemed in glory, it is grace all the way.

Mathematics students may understand this if I explain it in terms of an equation:

$$x + \infty = \infty$$

Any finite quantity x added to an infinite quantity ∞ will always yield infinity as its result. In fact, any operation of a finite quantity on an infinite quantity will yield infinity.

Our righteousness on earth is always a finite quantity. There will always be a "but" to limit its extent. But justification is an infinite quantity. It is a sovereign act of God towards ultimate redemption on the final day. It is so packaged that "neither death nor life, neither angels nor demons, neither the present nor the future, nor any powers, neither height nor depth, nor anything else in all creation will be able to separate us from the love of God that is in Christ Jesus our Lord" (Rom. 8:38–39), if we believe to the end (Matt. 10:22). If we use our mathematical equation and add our righteousness to justification as a basis for attaining resurrection, the equation reminds us that we are only resurrected because of our justification.

At first glance the idea of being resurrected only if we attain some level of holiness looks harmless, and possibly even beneficial: after all, it keeps people on their toes. That may be why preachers seldom discuss it. But the harm that this idea does is that it reintroduces the idea of law. Those who believe it live in fear again, because they are not sure of their place in heaven until they die. They endure life-long insecurity about their salvation.

Fear is the exact opposite of faith, and hence this teaching gnaws at a vital factor in their salvation. Holders of such views do not mature in the knowledge of Christ because they spend their energies in the cold grip of fear. They do not patiently walk with the Spirit to be remoulded from the inside. Instead they struggle to match up to outward codes they make up in their minds. They are so busy with these codes that they do not have the right focus for the Spirit to operate. The genuine holiness worked out by the Holy Spirit from within, which involves growth in knowledge of Christ and conformity to him, is displaced by a commitment to meeting local, external codes.

The problem with this insecurity is not that it requires us to grow in holiness. Its real problem is that it teaches us that God keeps us here to grow in holiness till we are "glorifiable", and then grabs us away. But this is wrong. God does not keep us here to become glorifiable. As soon as we are justified, we are glorifiable. Once we are declared just and accepted by God, our place is reserved in the many mansions that Jesus is preparing for us.

Please note the exact words I have used here. I am not saying that God does not expect us to grow in holiness. He expects us to "be perfect, therefore, as your heavenly father is perfect" (Matt. 5:48). We are to "purify ourselves from everything that contaminates body and spirit, perfecting holiness out of reverence for God" (2 Cor. 7:1). But that is not "why" he keeps us here. That is "how" to go about the "why" he keeps us here. So we should give full attention to our spiritual growth.

What Use Is Sanctification?

If sanctification does not ripen us for heaven, what use is it? The answer is that it serves two very important purposes in the Christian's life:

- **It sustains our justification**

The Christian faith is based on truth. The Spirit of Jesus Christ that justifies the believer is also called the Spirit of truth. If after we come to the faith we keep on sinning deliberately, if we keep on contradicting the Spirit that justified us, the Spirit remains checked and is hindered in his operations in our lives. It was not for nothing that at the very beginning of the great redemption section of the Bible, God declared, "My Spirit will not contend with human beings forever, for they are mortal" (Gen. 6:3). The alternative translation of the word "mortal" in a footnote in the TNIV is "corrupt". Since sin is anti-God, it steals our hearts away from God until faith wanes to the point that we do not acknowledge God in truth anymore. If we keep on getting corrupt, the Spirit will not continue to contend with us; he will leave. But if we yield to the Spirit's sanctifying work, he will keep drawing us closer and closer to God. It will become more difficult for us to fall for the deceits and allures of sin and to turn away from God. This way, our justification is sustained and we gladly wait for the appearing of the Son.

Remember, the condition for glorification is that our faith remains on the last day. It is to be doubted that we can truly continue to trust in God without continuously being renewed and refreshed by sanctification. To say otherwise is to imply that whatever we learnt, whatever we experienced, whatever grace we received at the moment we came to faith in Christ is enough to last a lifetime. What hubris! We need more knowledge from studying our Bible, more pragmatic experience of the Christian life, and more and more grace for which we commit ourselves to prayer. Without sanctification we cannot remain in faith. This is why the Apostle Peter tells us to make our election sure by pursuing sanctification and adding virtues to our faith (2 Pet. 1:5–11).

- **It makes us more useful and usable in God's hands**

The other role of sanctification follows from the first: "if you possess these qualities in increasing measure, they will keep you from being ineffective and unproductive in your knowledge of our Lord Jesus Christ" (2 Peter 1:8). This is exactly why we are left on earth. God could have taken us away to himself as soon as we were saved, but instead "he has committed to us the message of reconciliation. We are therefore Christ's ambassadors, as though God were making his appeal through us", to tell the world: "Be reconciled to God" (2 Cor. 5:19–20).

Before Jesus died, he explained that he needed to go back to the Father so that the Spirit might come to indwell all believers with the power of God to proclaim the gospel to the entire world. When Jesus was on earth, he could not reach more than one place at a time. Now that his Spirit indwells believers, God is in us ministering the same gospel of Christ to all the different regions of the earth. Believers in different cultures, generations and circumstances are enabled by the Holy Spirit to apply the same gospel to the different needs, aspirations and hopes of their different contexts.

Jesus stated, "I chose you and appointed you so that you might go and bear fruit – fruit that will last" (John 15:16). The only way to carry out this commission is by continuously being sanctified. By sanctification we draw nearer God, we are more open to being used by the Spirit, our faith keeps growing, we are empowered to do exploits, and we drift further away from the deceit of Satan.

Once we have been admitted as holy in the presence of God, we are required to live like the holy people of God, so that our holiness will be fulfilled in the presence of other people. We are no longer to live as "enemies of the cross of Christ", the very cross that bought our pardon.

Chris Wright wrote about how this truth applied to Israel in the Old Testament:

> Israel's unique historical experience was not a ticket to a cosy state of privileged favouritism. Rather it laid upon them a missionary task and a moral responsibility. If they failed in these, then in a sense they fell back to the level of any other nation. They stood, like all nations and all humanity, before the bar of God's judgement, and their history by itself gave them no guaranteed protection.[1]

The same stands true for Christians today. Our calling does not permit us to continue in careless living, disorderliness and sin. It demands that we quit sin and be holy and alive to our paramount duty in life – reconciling people to God. Paul in writing to the Corinthians referred to believers as "those sanctified in Christ Jesus and called to be his holy people" (1 Cor. 1:2). And that is what we, too, are called to be.

Questions

1. What one word describes God's act that changes a sinner into a saint?
2. Describe justification. Are you sure you are justified?
3. What does the author call the breath of spiritual life?
4. How does faith demonstrate itself in an already justified life?
5. On what conditions will one be glorified?
6. What is the importance of sanctification in the justified life?

---

[1] Chris H. Wright, *Knowing Jesus Through the Old Testament* (London: Marshall Pickering, 1992), 41.

6

THE TROUBLES OF SINNING

Although we understand the call to holiness, and may want to pursue holiness, there is a problem. We still tend to have a short-term view, in which we think that sin benefits us. We are very susceptible to the lies of the devil, who paints evil so that it appears good and gratifying. He suggests that warnings to flee sin are really moves to tame us and make us fit some religious mould, some preconceived idea of what godly people should be like. Aren't the things we are being asked to avoid merely harmless pleasure and useful avenues for gain or self-assertion?

Satan loves to offer plausible excuses like this for the things we do. And we tend to agree with him, thinking of most of our sins as minor issues that God should really brush aside. But that is not how God sees them. So in this chapter, we will try to take a clear-eyed look at the real effects of sin.

Cosmic Treason

R. C. Sproul describes sin as "cosmic treason … against a perfectly pure Sovereign. It is an act of supreme ingratitude toward One to whom we owe everything, to the One who has given us life itself."[1] His statement is supported by an interesting story from the Old Testament that shows how God reacts when his people blithely give in to sin. In Numbers 22 to 24, we read about how a Moabite king tried to persuade a prophet called Balaam to curse the nation of Israel, the people God had chosen and justified. But what was revealed to Balaam was that God "has not

---

[1] R. C. Sproul, *The Holiness of God* (Illinois: Tyndale House, 1985), 151.

observed iniquity in Jacob, nor has he seen wickedness in Israel. The Lord his God is with him" (Num. 23:21 NKJV). Yes, this was speaking about those same Israelites who had been provoking God and Moses from day one of the Exodus from Egypt! As far as God was concerned, there was no evil found in them. Their sins were forgiven; their iniquities were covered. God had justified them, and no amount of satanic accusations would persuade God to allow them to be cursed. Such is the strength of God's justification!

But one's eager reading of this exhilarating account of the beauty of God's faithfulness in justification is rudely interrupted in chapter 25. Many of the Israelites abandoned the faith: "the men began to indulge in sexual immorality with Moabite women, who invited them to the sacrifices to their gods. The people ate the sacrificial meal and bowed down before these gods. So Israel joined in worshipping the Baal of Peor. And the Lord's anger burned against them" (Num. 25:1–3). They must have taken God's grace for granted and thought they could live as they liked. "After all", they must have thought, "the only credential we need to be acceptable to God is to be circumcised descendants of Abraham. He won't mind if we 'play' with Moabite women and their gods." God proved them wrong. He rejected them and struck down 24,000 of them in his anger.

It is very dangerous to start to think in terms like "God won't mind" or "God won't do anything about it". This attitude aroused God's anger against the men of Judah at a later time, when they assumed the Lord will do nothing about their ways, whether they were good or bad. (Zeph. 1:12).

Jude was referring to incidents like the one in Numbers when he wrote, "I want to remind you that the Lord at one time delivered his people out of Egypt, but later destroyed those who did not believe" (Jude 5). We all may be saved from the Egypt of sin. We all may join the band of those covered by the broad blanket of God's justification. But God will sort out those who do not believe, those who have joined in the exodus for some reason other than genuine faith. Their bodies may have come out of Egypt but they have left their hearts there. They show their unbelief by loving sin.

In Numbers 32:23 we are warned, "You may be sure that your sin will find you out." The writer of Hebrews was also referring to the failure of those Old Testament people who initially joined God's justified people in the Exodus but did not enter final redemption into Canaan when he warned us:

> Let us, therefore, make every effort to enter that rest, so that no one will fall by following their example of disobedience.
> For the word of God is alive and active. Sharper than any double-edged sword, it penetrates even to dividing soul and spirit, joints and marrow; it judges the thoughts and attitudes of the heart. Nothing in all creation is hidden from God's sight. Everything is uncovered and laid bare before the eyes of him to whom we must give account (Heb. 4:11–13).

Still today, God's word keeps searching out the intents and purposes of all hearts, sorting out those who will fall because of unbelief, those who came to the wedding ceremony without the wedding garment, those who go along with God's people but whose hearts are turned away from God.

What marks these people out is not the fact that they fall into sin, but the fact that they prefer to keep on indulging their old sinful nature. They prefer sin to righteousness and self to God. This is the unfailing marker that distinguishes belief from unbelief. Those who truly believe in God will always prefer to struggle against sin; the others prefer the comfort of compromising to avoid the struggle. They may attempt to explain it away, but their commitment to self largely overwhelms any genuine commitment to God.

Human beings were created to "rule over … every living creature" (Gen. 1:28–30) and we are determined to do this. Medical science can now help those suffering from infertility; advances in communication have given us e-mail, the Internet and satellite systems that have expanded the frontiers of knowledge; advances in genetic engineering are providing hope for those suffering from previously incurable diseases and are tackling the problem of aging. Some see this as offering hope of the elimination of death! No wonder humanity seems to be positioning itself to take over from God.

But our ability to rule nature is not matched by an ability to rule ourselves. We are still ruled by instincts and impulses that incapacitate us when it comes to contending with sin. We fear shame, pain and sorrow.

Such fear can only be countered by strong convictions that are not used to explain away issues but that have been submitted to the rigorous test of God's word.

Sin demeans us before our neighbours. It makes us mean and parochial because it encourages us to trample on others in order to advance ourselves. It makes us critical of others for sins that we tolerate in ourselves.

> This basic self-centeredness affects all our behaviour. We do not find it easy to adjust to other people. We tend either to despise them or to envy them, to have either superiority or inferiority feelings. For we seldom think of ourselves with that 'sober judgement' which Paul urged upon his readers. Sometimes we are full of self-pity, at other times of self-esteem, self-will or self-love.
>
> Most quarrels are due to a misunderstanding, and the misunderstanding is due to our failure to appreciate the other man's point of view. It is more natural to us to talk than to listen, to argue than to submit ... conflicts could be resolved if both sides first examined themselves critically, and then examined the other side charitably.[2]

Unfortunately, conflicts continue, distrust reigns, estranged relationships abound, evil escalates, and our world is distorted because of sin.

Sin Did Not Pay in the Past

The garden was lush green, the environment was serene. It was the sort of setting millionaires long for. Everything was in its right place. The man had an ideally suited younger woman for a partner and they were alone in the expansive property, bordered on all sides by clear running water with no trace of industrial pollution. But they gave in to sin. And that was all it took to turn that whole beautiful scene upside down.

This couple who were supervising all that God had made and managing it while God smiled on them suddenly shrank away from God because of the cold chill of sin. When the idea of sinning first flashed

---

[2] John R. W. Stott, *Basic Christianity* (Illinois: InterVarsity Press, 1971), 78–79.

across their minds, their hearts must have turned from it in revulsion. But when the idea returned, their fear and disgust ebbed. The idea began to consume their minds, until it gained possession of their hearts and became irresistible. They gave in to the struggle, sank below the surface and drank from the mire.

The Bible records the state of their minds before and after they sinned. Genesis 2:25 records, "The man and his wife were both naked, and they felt no shame". Shame is a variant of fear. It is the fear of social censure due to a consciousness of unworthiness, real or imagined, caused by some disgrace or reproach. With God on their side, this couple were free from shame. They were secure in their minds and not afraid of anyone's opinion. Even though they were physically undressed, they were properly dressed spiritually. They were therefore not afraid in the presence of God.

But as soon as they sinned, Adam said to God, "I heard you in the garden, and I was afraid because I was naked; so I hid" (Gen. 3:10). He started hiding from God. Instead of jumping into the arms of his source, his author and his provider, he ran. His link with God had snapped. It was not really his physical nakedness that bothered him, it was his spiritual nakedness. He had been lowered in position and was now fleeing from the source of "every good and perfect gift" (James 1:17).

If he was fleeing from good, it is only reasonable to assume that he was fleeing towards evil. He was running from life to death, from abundance to poverty, from health to sickness. Sin had reproached him. He felt guilty and unworthy and knew he had made himself an enemy. He had not acted as a son ought to his father. He and Eve were brought low by the same sin that had promised to raise them to be like God. How much better things would have been if they had taken steps to win that battle!

King David was someone else who destroyed the bountiful life of peace and providence that God had packaged for him. He was God's chosen king, and the peoples' too. He sought God's heart to please him. He rose from the ashes and became a colossus. But Satan does not withdraw from battle just because someone has come close to God. Instead, he doubles his efforts. David had won many, many struggles aimed at pulling him into sin, especially when he spared the life of Saul (1 Sam. 24, 26). He nearly succumbed to the temptation to murder

Nabal, Abigail's husband, but the Holy Spirit calmed his rage through Abigail's wisdom (1 Sam. 25:1–38). Nevertheless, the devil came back to tempt him again, and he proved vulnerable. For a moment David lost his orientation. Instead of remembering that his security was in God, he allowed his mind to enjoy the security of his wealth as he looked out over his kingdom from the roof of his palace.

Palace roofs seem to have been dangerous places! Many centuries later, Nebuchadnezzar the king of Babylon was walking on his roof when he too got carried with pride in the city spread out before him. God quickly drove him out to dwell with the beasts of the field for seven years (Dan. 4:29).

David's heart was filled with pride. When he saw the beautiful body of a naked woman it fitted into his consciousness of his achievements – the great structures he had built, his agricultural programmes and the peace that pervaded Jerusalem. A resonance was set up that amplified his sense of power. His thoughts may have been very similar to those of Nebuchadnezzar centuries later. "Is not this the great [Jerusalem] I have built as the royal residence, by my mighty power and for the glory of my majesty" (Dan. 4:30). He saw the woman as part of his property, which he had the sovereign right to enjoy. He appropriated the glory due to God and fell into sin, defiling another man's wife.

You can trust the deceiver to really mess people up. Of all the nights that David could have been tempted in the month, it was only on this night, when the woman was ovulating so that she would be likely to get pregnant, that David was tempted. He fell and had to face the shame that his adultery would soon be public knowledge. He struggled to keep it secret, but soon it came down to two choices: his honour or Uriah's life. He fell further as he murdered the man he had cheated (2 Sam. 11). The struggle did not end there. Would David continue in pride and reject God's judgement, delivered to him by Nathan? Thankfully, David realized that he was slipping very fast into destruction and fell before God in complete contrition.

Despite all the promises David had received from God, all the love that God had showered on him, sin had kick-started trouble in his life. This adultery led to murder so he could cover it up. He did evil in the sight of God, and the Lord responded:

Now, therefore, the sword will never depart from your house, because you despised me and took the wife of Uriah the Hittite to be your own.

… Out of your own household I am going to bring calamity upon you. Before your very eyes I will take your wives and give them to one who is close to you, and he will sleep with your wives in broad daylight. You did it in secret, but I will do this thing in broad daylight before all Israel (2 Sam. 12:10–12).

The Lord forgave David when he repented, just as he forgives each of us when we unconditionally repent from an evil we have done. He does not do this if our repentance is like that of King Saul, who wanted to repent but still hung onto his honour: "I have sinned. But please honour me before the elders of my people and before Israel; come back with me, so that I may worship the Lord your God" (1 Sam. 15:30). Despite his sin, Saul still wanted to be honoured. He sought to use Samuel's company at worship as a political tool to keep his people united behind him. God saw through such repentance and utterly rejected his kingdom and withdrew from him.

Yet even though God forgave David, he did not prevent the repercussions of his sins. First, the child of the misconduct died. Then evil continued to multiply in David's household. His son raped his daughter, and became a permanent example of failure to distinguish lust from love (2 Sam. 13:1–19). Absalom, probably the son David loved most, brought trouble to the house of David till his own sins sent him to his grave too early. He murdered Amnon, his half-brother who had raped Tamar his sister, and named his own daughter after the raped girl, possibly to keep him in remembrance of the evil. He fled into exile, but returned two years later and spent four years luring the hearts of the Israelites away from his father before staging a mutiny that threatened to unseat David. Absalom even added incest to his crimes, sleeping with his father's mistresses in an orgy arranged and advertised by his deputies to convince his followers that there was no possibility of reconciliation with his father (2 Sam. 13–18).

Nor did the evil end with Absalom's death. Infighting, intrigues and betrayals marked the rest of David's reign. There was so much trouble that in his old age another of his sons attempted to snatch the throne from him. David brought momentary respite by vacating the throne for one of his youngest sons, Solomon (1 Kgs. 1). He died the only Israelite king to have vacated the throne alive, without reason of impairment, just to avoid the bloodletting that would follow if he hung onto the throne till death. The succession was organized in haste and set one of his sons against another, leading to the death of one son so that the other could consolidate his hold on the throne.

Sin had terrible consequences for the most golden home in the land of Israel. What would have happened if David had not given in to that three-fold sin – pride in his achievements, adultery with Bathsheba, and the murder of Uriah? He might have suffered momentary discomfort at not being able to gratify the flesh with its desires. But that would have been it. Instead he got a lifetime of trouble for a pleasure that was over in minutes.

Sin never pays. It is not just something we do; it is something that has licence to bring further evil upon us once we submit to it. We must flee it!

Sin Does Not Pay in the Present

We all know of people who have been brought low by sin. In your own neighbourhood it may not be difficult to find someone who bears a mark of disgrace or to remember someone who was killed and left behind an unfulfilled dream of a brilliant life. The person may have been very talented – a sportsman, an academic, an artist, a journalist, an engineer or the like. In fact, without previously thinking of it, I suddenly realize that I have examples of people in each of the above professions whose lives were soured by sin.

There was the local science teacher, an expert in chemistry, who died of acid burns when a young woman he had been dating took revenge for his broken promise to marry her. There was the journalist, quite brilliant in his good days, who became an alcoholic and was drunk almost every time we saw him. He was demoted from one position to another, until he was eventually fired. There was the engineer with a promising future who developed a liking for drugs, which ended his career because he could no longer reason clearly. There was the Nigerian international footballer in the mid-eighties who never obeyed camp rules and was all over town with women. He was shot in the thigh a few weeks before a major competition in Chile in 1987. He recovered just as the tournament was about to start. Thereafter he went to Belgium to play professionally, but his indiscipline persisted. He eventually fled home to Nigeria when he was convicted of raping an underage girl, and months later was also convicted of being in possession of hard drugs. He lived the rest of his life in Nigeria to avoid going to jail in Europe. Professional football? He never really played again.

Two musicians of international repute, the reggae king and the Afrobeat king, died because of their excesses. Robert Nester Marley, a Jamaican reggae legend, insisted on smoking marijuana until he died of cancer in 1981 at the age of 36. Fela Anikulapo Kuti, a Nigerian Afrobeat maestro, combined marijuana smoking with impudent womanizing until he died of AIDS in 1997.

Many others, businessmen, politicians and preachers, live at only half of their potential today or have been completely wiped out because of sin. It is not to be imagined that all these people started indulging in the sins that destroyed them without some inner struggle. But they all gave in to the pressure at some time and started making excuses for their behaviour. They may well have dismissed warnings from others who were sincerely concerned about them with thoughts like, "Why should I quit? Who are they to dictate to me?"

They may even cite science to support their behaviour. This is one tactic the devil is using to sell homosexuality by claiming that it is genetically determined. So God is to blame for someone's choosing to practise it. It is a pity that this lie is even being propagated from some pulpits. If homosexuality is genetic, then so are most other sexual practices. Traditional Africans must be right when they claim that God created African men to marry more than one wife – after all, it's genetic! Scientists would do even better to confirm that sin itself is genetic. How else could the phenomenon that sin passed from Adam to the entire world be explained biologically? Yet God calls us to quit sin, and he has provided the means for us to do so.

Americans still remember President Richard Nixon. He probably had more reasons not to fail the way he did than any American president before him, for God had given him his trusted prophet Billy Graham as a confidant. But the devil drove him to hang on to power by any means, and the resulting Watergate scandal swept him out of office.

We still remember the irrepressible Samuel Doe of Liberia, who was so ebullient and full of life. He hung on to power by unjust means, sucked the nation dry, and felt like a god over Liberia. He was eventually captured by Yormie Johnson, a man who could probably never have won an election against Doe if Doe had opened up the government to real democracy and sincere leadership. Doe was stripped naked before a village community and slowly hacked to death. How are the mighty fallen!

Sin? It never pays! In Africa, there are many like Samuel Doe. Corruption, evil, ungodliness and utter wickedness are hallmarks of their manner of governance. In the twenty-first century, they still hope to benefit from wrongdoing. They appear never to learn from the fate of the former rulers they hold captive today. It would be wise for them to learn that their security is only guaranteed if the populace feels secure from hunger, nakedness and social, political and economic repression. They do not appear to have learnt that the leader of today will necessarily be the citizen of tomorrow, and that if those who take over the reins of leadership follow their own example, there will be still more bloodletting.

Public figures are not always perceived as real people when we talk about them. There is a feeling that they are issues or ideas, but not persons. But the truth is that public figures are just like us. The evil or good we discuss in them is also found in us; the only difference is that they are unfortunate enough to be facing the glare of publicity. We face the same types of temptations and the same struggles in life as they do. Their greed may attract public attention, but ours is private. Their lust and pride are analyzed publicly, but ours hide with us in our little corners. However, the truth remains that God is equally concerned with their sins and ours. We must, therefore, invest a lot of effort in ensuring that we do not yield to the flesh and self, lest we suffer the same reproaches and fate.

A number of the problems we are facing now could be a direct result of our sin. Maybe you are hiding from an old friend because you lied to or cheated him or her. Sin is cutting you short. There is a home somewhere today where the family is polarized between the father and mother. Sin triggered it, maybe using an abusive father or a nagging mother. Their joy in a peaceful home is being denied by Satan. Gangs in the United States and European cities and cult members in Nigerian universities shoot, maim and kill members of rival groups to such an extent that members avoid being in the streets alone – but these people joined their gangs in order to "enjoy life to the fullest". Now they live with their hearts in their mouths, afraid of the police, society and rival gang members. Today they live in hate, sorrow and terror. There is somebody somewhere who is deeply disturbed, not because she has no clothes, but because someone in her neighbourhood dresses in clothes she cannot afford. All day long she is filled with sorrow and may soon end up in another sin to ensure that she wears similar dresses. Somewhere there is a church where attendance is steadily decreasing or whose doors have closed because of the sins of the elders and parsons. How many church people in your city have joined a secret society or a mafia group in order to make money? Do you think they enjoy their wealth? Truly there is no peace for the wicked. Sin does not pay!

How many pastors have, at one time or other, been drawn back to sort out the events of their Friday evening half-way into preparing Sunday's sermon? The preparation of the sermon had been flowing truly as a dew from heaven, but suddenly, like a bolt from the blue, yesterday's event broke in to interrupt the flow from on high. That flow must stop until the preacher leaves the table and kneels to sort out the previous day. What a painful experience! Yet sadly some pastors are professionals at ignoring the call to repentance. They forgo the flow from on high and water down their sermons in order not to face their sins of yesterday.

All of us need to face up to the truth that sin is destructive and demeaning; it perverts the real meaning of life and warps life itself. In place of honour, sin brings dishonour; in place of strength, it produces weakness. Sin brings down; it never exalts. Those who have made gains by sin will ultimately lose even what they started with. Sin destroys good neighbourliness and in its place plants mutual suspicion and strife. Above all, sin keeps us estranged from God. When we should feel free to approach him for help, our sin keeps us away from him in fear instead of faith.

For all these reasons, we ought to strive to keep ourselves from sin. The pain and shame we may suffer now in our struggle against sin may be disheartening, but the consequences we may have to bear if we do give in will be far worse than what we are now enduring.

Questions

1. Has there been any time when sin reproached you? Explain.
2. Why do people not want to give up sin?
3. Identify a relationship problem you are having. What actions on your own part have contributed to it?
4. What are you doing to solve the problem?

7

COMMON STRUGGLES
CHRISTIANS FACE TODAY

Many years ago in places like the United Kingdom it was fashionable to be a Christian. It was a thing of pride to talk of being committed to missionary work in places like Asia, Africa and Latin America. How things have changed! The old values have been eroded. Today it is acceptable to send material aid to the majority world, but it must be sent without any reference to the name of Christ who taught us to love our neighbours.

This change has led some to assert that Christians today face more difficult inner struggles than those of the last generation. The truth is that all our struggles have been experienced by others before us. The only thing we lack today is community support, which means that we must now become like the Christians of the first century and learn to stand on our own feet.

Most of our struggles stem from two factors: first, how much of life's truth we know, which affects how easily we are deceived by Satan's lies, and secondly, how much we still live for self rather than for God and others.

The struggle between our desires for self-esteem, financial and material possessions and gratification of the flesh and our commitment to Christ will be greatly reduced if we take more and more of Christ into our lives. Initially the path will be difficult and the obstacles may seem insurmountable, but as we persist despite failures and feed on Christ, the frequency of our struggles will start to decline. However, we should not mistake a reduction in frequency for complete victory: attacks will still come, as they did in David's case, and they may be even more lethal because our guard is down.

I keep hoping that every Christian will learn and accept that this tension will last a lifetime. The devil and our sinful nature are constantly working to make us turn away from Christ. They will use different techniques – blackmail, seduction, persecution, threatening of the spirit, soul or body – but regardless of the technique, if they get us to turn away from Christ, they have won. But if we cling to Christ, trusting him to take away our sins and to fill us with righteousness until the end, we have won.

It is worth taking some time to look at some common conflict areas so that we are better able to identify the often-subtle temptations that are put in our path.

Money Matters

Money matters are complex. Even Scripture acknowledges this, for it says that "money is the answer for everything" (Eccl. 10:19) and that "the love of money is a root of all kinds of evil" (1 Tim. 6:10). It is this combination of the need for money and the love of it (especially when we love it more than our neighbours) that produces subtle temptations. We are as likely to be tempted when we do not have enough money as when we do.

Our insecurity about whether things will continue as they are leads us to try to use the resources available to us today to create a financial buffer against disasters that may lie ahead. This becomes a problem when either because of poverty or wealth we end up trusting money to determine our fate. We may also accumulate large amounts while some of our poor neighbours languish and perish without our noticing. We may even end up valuing people on the basis of what we know they own.

If we attach a high value to money, we are likely to spend our lives chasing it. We will be subtly tempted as our love for money competes with our love for others. Whether we are in ministry or business, we will be confronted with decisions in which we have to weigh people against money. The choice may be between providing decent wages for your staff or growing your business rapidly. It may be between keeping your promise to repay a debt or seizing a once-in-a-lifetime investment opportunity that promises quick returns. It may be between delivering the quality of job ordered or supplying something of almost the same quality to save a few coins. It could even be between selling a lucrative item that is destructive to its users (e.g. hard drugs) or less lucrative but healthier goods.

A key to victory in our financial struggles is to lift our eyes off our wallets, or the dream house, or the other things that money could buy and fix our eyes on the Lord Jesus. Doing this lightens our burden and neutralizes our illusions and the charm of money. It can also be helpful to take time to pray and possibly seek the counsel of a mature, Spirit-filled Christian in cases where we are facing a particularly difficult financial choice.

Attitudes to Work

Some contradictions of Christianity are also found in the way Christian artisans and professionals go about their jobs. It is very important that we should put our best into anything we are paid for. Technicians should never see their workshops as entirely private concerns in which they are the overlords.

The natural expectation would be that a Christian's business should blossom as he or she grows in faith. As the person demonstrates growing honesty, genuine concern for others, and seriousness in what they do, people would want to patronize their business. Unfortunately this is rarely the case, and the reason is not obscure. It is that many of us still fall short on the character traits that draw customers.

Some Christians are still struggling with lack of character. Others start enjoying Christian fellowship and spend too much of their time at church, sparing less attention for their business. Business never grows this way. Our churches should find ways to moderate church activities so that workers can find enough time to attend to their businesses and build integrity in the workplace. This also is an avenue for evangelism. People never love to patronize a good worker who is rarely seen.

It brings down businesses and brings reproach to the name of Christ when Christian professionals, artisans and businessmen can rarely be trusted with money, good jobs, and timely delivery. Such behaviour quickly erodes all efforts to portray Christ to the public in a good light. Those who pay us for jobs must be given their money's worth, they must be listened to, and we should do our best to satisfy them and to convince them that we have done what ought to have been done.

The temptations that arise due to unfaithfulness in the workplace can be avoided by reminding ourselves that even our apparently secular work is being done for the Lord (Col. 3:23–24). Those of us who are in public service should be exemplary workers.

Of course, sometimes a Christian's uprightness in the workplace may bring them hatred, envy and persecution by their fellow-workers. If this happens to you, do not seek to escape such troubles except, where possible, righteously. Take heart from the words of 1 Peter 4:16: "However, if you suffer as a Christian, do not be ashamed, but praise God that you bear that name".

Being Out of Touch

How good we feel about the things we do should never be used to judge how well we are doing in God's sight. Unfortunately we all fall for that idea. A very satisfied student once told me how members of his church maintain holy standards. He boasted that they were encouraged to stop attending community meetings because alcoholic drinks were served and unwholesome words were uttered when disagreements arose about community issues. But, I wondered, if Christians keep away from such meetings, who is there to encourage and challenge people to improve their lives? Cursing, drinking and swearing will be taken as the norm! We are God's candles, and candles are meant to be used in dark places, not reserved for use in daylight.

The more Christians do not seek genuine opportunities to interact positively with unbelievers, the more our vision of evangelism remains only a dream. Those of us who cannot participate in events with unbelievers without falling should cry for grace to grow so as to be able to be "in the world and not of the world". Is it not rather absurd for a Christian who has lost touch with the world he was commissioned to reach for Christ to boast of how aloof he is to his calling?

A superficial style of nonconformity is the classical pharisaical trap. The kingdom of God is not about wearing buttons, movies, or dancing. The concern of God is not focused on what we eat or what we drink. The call of nonconformity is a call to a deeper level of righteousness that goes beyond externals. When piety is defined exclusively in terms of externals the whole point of the teaching of the apostles has been lost. Somehow we have failed to hear the words of Jesus that it is not what goes into a man's mouth that defiles a man, but what comes out of his mouth. We still want to make the kingdom a matter of eating and drinking.

Why are such distortions rampant in Christian circles? The only answer I can give is sin. Our marks of piety can actually be evidences of impiety. When we major in minors and blow insignificant trifles out of proportions, we imitate the Pharisees. When we make dancing and movies the test of spirituality, we are guilty of substituting a cheap morality for a genuine one. We do these things to obscure the deeper issues of righteousness. Anyone can avoid dancing or going to movies. These require no great effort of moral courage. What is difficult is to control the tongue, to act with integrity, to show forth the fruit of the Spirit.[1]

It is time we stopped feeding our ignorance and selfish recalcitrance and applied our minds and hands to really touch people. We must reach out to the unreached nations and peoples and maintain the genuine gospel among the untouched people of the reached people groups. The unfeigned gospel must be maintained for coming generations.

One reason evangelism ranks lowest in our list of concerns today is possibly because we have lost Christ. In the West we have bought into Christ's call for others' welfare and human rights. In much of enlightened Africa we have accepted his socialism, but in both places we have largely lost the missionary Christ.

Our struggles with the lures of a cushion-Christianity can be overcome by radically feeding on and responding to the Jesus of the Bible. If we

---

[1] R. C. Sproul, *The Holiness of God* (Illinois: Tyndale House, 1985), 207–208.

allow him to live out his life in us, he will evangelize through us. "What will my friends say?" is Satan's coinage for worrying about what our enemies will say. We should wonder more about what Jesus will say when with so many resources today we do so little for the souls of men. We ought to worry when democracy and human rights are pushed to the precipice of individualism, so that now everyone is encouraged to hold onto whatever they choose to believe, because "we all believe in one god or another, and all gods are ultimately the same". How can we stand aloof?

Religiosity and Good Samaritans

One lesson Jesus' story of the Good Samaritan in Luke 10 teaches is that our religiosity does not guarantee us God's approval at all times. We must moment by moment seek out and do his will.

Impediments to demonstrating the love of God often arise because we are dealing with difficult human traditions or trying to meet other peoples' expectations, either in the church or in secular society. Often we fear what either our fellow-believers or society may say. But God's real interest is not in our keeping religious codes but that in relating with our neighbours, we love them. Our actions and inactions towards others must stem from genuine love for them. God demands altruism. We should never hold others in disdain or even call our neighbour, "you fool", even in our minds.

Come to think of it, are you genuinely interested in the poor and hurting? Would you step out of your security zone to help them? Are you positively involved in uplifting them? If you are someone who sets or carries out policies, do you ensure equal opportunities for all? It is not too late to start.

The socially underprivileged – whether by race or status – are included in the "poor". And the Bible says, "whoever oppresses the poor shows contempt for their Maker, but whoever is kind to the needy honours God" (Prov. 14:31). It takes spirituality to hurt with those that hurt, to feel lack with those that lack, to feel pain with those that suffer. It takes the love of God – and that alone is religion acceptable to God.

> Is not this the kind of fasting I have chosen: to loose the chains of injustice and untie the cords of the yoke, to set the oppressed free and break every yoke? Is it not to share your food with the hungry and to provide the poor wanderer with shelter – when you see the naked, to clothe them, and not to turn away from your own flesh and blood? … If you do away with the yoke of oppression, with the pointing finger and malicious talk, and if you spend yourselves in behalf of the hungry and satisfy the needs of the oppressed, then your light will rise in the darkness, and your night will become like the noonday (Isa. 58:6–10).

These words reveal what makes the Good Samaritan tick. If we are to receive God's commendation, we must offer to share in the sufferings of the deprived. Our ego is going to complain that we are bending too low, but once again we need to look at Jesus. He was prepared to step down from heaven to earth, to move from glory to dishonour, from life to death, in order to save us. The gap we have to bridge is only that between one human being and another. Yet sadly it takes a struggle for us to meet others at their places of need.

Nursing Wounded Soldiers

There are other spiritual lessons that can be drawn from the story of the Good Samaritan. One is that sometimes our fellow-believers fall into the hands of the enemy and are wounded and robbed by the evil one. They almost immediately become pariahs, unacceptable Samaritans to us "Jews". A struggle ensues to love those who have fallen into sin and deal with them in love while trying to rescue and heal them. It is easier to brand the fallen as enemies who must be disgraced and discredited. Those who sin may have to be punished, but the purpose for which we apply punishment matters. Are we aiming solely to punish or to correct? Are we sensitive to those who are truly repentant or do we come down on them with the full force of the law?

Paul noted that dealing with Christians who have sinned is a source of strong temptations. He warned the Galatian church: "Brothers and sisters, if someone is caught in a sin, you who live by the Spirit should restore that person gently. But watch yourselves, or you also may be tempted" (Gal. 6:1). I suspect this is one of the most unheeded warnings of Scripture! If our dealing with those who have fallen is motivated by anything short of love, or for any purpose other than to restore them, we have failed.

Another source of temptation the apostle noted is that we will struggle with unwillingness to "carry each other's burdens" (Gal. 6:2). When one of us hurts as part of the body, each of us should respond in love. We should not keep aloof. Of course, it is not always easy to find out why the person fell. Those who sin do not always appear weak; they at times tend to look stubborn or tough, but that is only a cover as their humiliated minds rebuff blame. We should learn to look beyond this veneer of strength to see the weakness within and find a humble means to counsel and encourage those who fail. Again, in saying this I am not saying that it may not sometimes be necessary to punish someone in order to correct them.

The third source of temptation is comparing ourselves with the one who sinned. That makes us feel good because we imagine that in the same circumstances we would have done better (Gal. 6:3–4). But that is not necessarily true. Thus Paul instructs Christians to be content to weigh their own actions against the word of God. The mere attempt to compare ourselves favourably with someone else is a pointer to how unspiritual we are and how far we still have to go spiritually.

We are not to overlook sin and pretend that all is well when someone falls into sin. Such dishonesty makes the condition even worse than explicit antagonism would. But whatever our reaction, we must constantly keep in mind what fallen Christians will become when they outgrow their failures, for the God "who began a good work in [them] will carry it on to completion until the day of Christ Jesus" (Phil. 1:6).

Criticism and Tale-Bearing

Criticism has been a major issue for leaders and followers since the dawn of time. It is very easy to criticize. All it takes is the flimsiest of excuses, a minimal expense of energy through the tongue, and possibly a listening ear. It is also a very pleasurable exercise. It creates a feeling of conviviality and camaraderie, albeit momentarily, between the critics.

But if there is anything that destroys societies it is the pointing finger and malicious talk. Imagine how you would feel if, for instance, you had spent long hours doing some duty in the church. Then you were criticized and told that your zeal was a ploy to get attention and that you were trying to outdo someone whose assistance you were grateful for. This is the kind of treatment church leaders constantly suffer. It has driven many vibrant Christians back into their shells. Some have left because they imagine that it must be outright hatred that has led people to concoct such lies and sustain them with so much gusto that even the most spiritual in the church have believed them.

The ugly thing about criticism and gossip is that those who initiate them feel they have done nothing because they "were just talking and didn't expect it to go any further". Others say, "I was only suggesting a possibility; maybe I used the wrong words", and so on. These are very flimsy excuses for such destructive actions.

Gossip is malicious talk about someone else. It is rampant even among Christians because it is the easiest and seemingly most harmless way we can get back at those who have upset us. Nearly everyone falls into this dangerous trap. Why do we gossip? It is because we hate, envy, or at least do not love enough to tolerate waiting for an opportunity to lovingly discuss the situation with the person we are criticizing and give them an opportunity to explain what is going on.

It was only recently that I myself came to terms with the truth that anyone who can control the tongue is already perfect (James 3:2). Years ago, I thought that the greatest problem was doing away with lust. Now I know better. We are all susceptible to the base attitudes that kick-start hatred and criticisms within our minds and that later find expression in gossip.

Some who criticize do so because they feel some personal lack of fulfilment that they blame directly or indirectly on the one they are criticizing. Some criticize not because the object of their criticism did any obvious evil but because they want to raise themselves in other peoples' eyes. But regardless of whether criticism springs from an inferiority complex that drives us to run others down, a superiority complex that provokes us to climb over them, or even from outright hatred, it is a serious flaw. We must not yield to the common temptation to speak evil about others. We must watch out when we find ourselves filing away in our minds the wrong things a brother or sister has been doing or the privileges he or she has not been according us. Beware! Our sinful nature is planning to run someone down. The danger of criticism is that it infects both the critic and the hearers. It may be the dynamite the devil has been waiting for to blow up God's church. Beware!

The Bible warns, "The tongue also is a fire, a world of evil among the parts of the body. It corrupts the whole person, sets the whole course of one's life on fire, and is itself set on fire by hell" (James 3:6). It also says "Those who guard their lips preserve their lives, but those who speak rashly will come to ruin" (Prov. 13:3). It was in responding to unfair criticism that Jesus mentioned that some sins may never be forgiven (Matt. 12:22–37). In a stringent warning against careless use of the tongue, he said, "But I tell you that people will have to give account on the day of judgement for every empty word they have spoken" (Matt. 12:36).

The list of those brought down by the misuse of the tongue is endless. Miriam, Moses' brave elder sister, became leprous when she unjustly criticized the humble servant of God (Num. 12). Korah and his company were respected leaders amongst the children of Israel, but they were swallowed up by the earth because of their criticism (Num. 16). Michal, David's wife, was barren for life for criticizing the king who danced before the Lord (2 Sam. 6:16–23). The church in Corinth needed the special attention of the Apostle Paul to put them back on track when they turned critical, with each party taking swipes at the apostles who had brought some of them to faith (1 Cor. 1:10–12; 2 Cor. 10).

Sexual Relationships

The deceitfulness of sexual sin is the stuff of legend. Yet although it has done incalculable harm to multitudes through history, others still pursue it as though sex is worth living for.

Why do we often slide into struggles with sexual temptation? Well, do you like watching God's artwork – muscular men, slim women, robust girls, long legs, etc.? Do you feel excitement at their different shapes and sizes? If your answer is yes, you need to start instructing your mind that there is nothing extraordinarily different between one person and another, or you may be vulnerable to voyeurism. Does what you see of the opposite sex pervade your mind so that you long for private and intimate moments so you can see, hear and feel the person? Start now to warn your mind to desist from focusing on people's physical bodies and desiring their company because of what they look like. Remember that the physical body is merely the human casing, and can be extremely deceitful. The real person is what is inside that casing.

Sexual sin is rampant because it is accessible to all. No matter how poor they are, every boy, girl, man or woman has what it takes to fall into sexual sin. The poor are tempted because sex is a way to have fun and feel loved in a harsh world. The rich are tempted because sex is a gratifier of achievers. The attraction of sex is also not easily resistible as it appeals to our most primordial instincts. Strangers need only see each other regularly, talk about ordinary things when they meet, and do nothing to tame their personal feelings for each other, and the next moment they are plunged into sexual sin.

One reason we are so upset by sexual sin is its consequences both here on earth and in the hereafter. Even the wise King Solomon allowed his unbridled quest for women to drag him into flagrant idolatry until his heart was weaned away from God. The truth is that sexual sin is not only harmful; it also defaces the meaning of human life.

Voyeurism is an increasing problem these days. Christians who appear to hate sexual sin still find pleasure in watching pornography and spend their money on it. But those who service the pornography industry, whether live or on screen, are self-destructing. If we loved them, we would deny that industry all the money we can control till they are too short of funds to lure more young people into their ranks. Romans 1:32 is very useful here: "Although they know God's righteous decree that those who do such things deserve death, they not only continue to do these very things but also approve of those who practise them." If something is wrong, do not patronize its production; that is God's standard.

Sexual sin has brought untold reproach to multitudes. Samson, the superman of Israel, died a blinded prisoner because he could not control his sexual appetites (Judg. 16). Prince Charles and the late Lady Diana brought shame to the British monarchy with the accounts of their sexual escapades. Former American president Bill Clinton is remembered less for his political achievements than for having risked his family and job for a taste of Monica Lewinsky's flesh. In 1998 the news was everywhere that Justin Fashanu, the first black player to ever hit the million pound mark in a transfer deal in the English Premier League, had taken his own life, leaving a slew of reports of improper sexual activities and drug addiction.

The lives of many young people have been stunted because they were misled into sex while they should still have been undergoing training for full adulthood. Many girls never achieve their potential because they have to drop out of school to raise their children alone.

Consider also the heartaches of the broken homes that often stem from illicit sexual involvement. Sex has the innate power to bind a couple strongly together in a purposeful union. It binds them even more as they become committed to their children, who are the personification and result of their union. Yet sex also has the capacity to destroy people who abuse it.

Christians who are of marriageable age should be encouraged to marry, according to the Bible. But the problem is that sexual urges start earlier than the normal marriage ages these days. Consequently even those still in school are not immune to this temptation.

Much sexual temptation simmers in the environment to which we are exposed – the company we keep, what we see, hear or read. We should thus learn to jealously guard our hearts and to open them only in edifying environments. Unguarded TV-watching exposes us to the lures for sexual sin by showing the unlimited imaginations of warped minds. But there are also many other techniques that Satan uses to hoodwink us. He will suggests that sex offers some new magic thrill when you enjoy partners of different shapes, sizes and ages. That is the devil's lie. Learn to be contented. When once you believe the devil's lies, you will spend the rest of your life chasing after the magic thrill that ever eludes you. It is a question of what you let your mind believe.

Fellowship with other Christians, Bible study, prayer and meditation are all potent ways of cleansing the heart of impure thoughts. It is also important that you be satisfied with who you are. Do not try to bolster your sense of self-worth by seeking intimacy with the other sex. Such a solution to your insecurity will only bring you a world of troubles.

Faithfulness to the Word

Unfaithfulness to the word of God and general lassitude when it comes to serious Bible study, interpretation and purposeful preaching is a sin of today's church. A generation of Christians has emerged who quote with absolute assurance passages that soothe their nerves. But with the arrogance that should be reserved for unbelievers, they overrule the Bible when a passage does not suit their purposes.

Contextual preaching is fast being flushed away by those who pick phrases, clauses or even single words or statements out of Scripture and build doctrines around their private interests, without any thought about what the words meant in their context. God mandates preaching, but preaching must start with proper preparation. As Paul told Timothy, "Do your best to present yourself to God as one approved, a worker who does not need to be ashamed and who correctly handles the word of truth" (2 Tim. 2:15).

The message of the Bible is addressed to a believing and worshipping people, not a coterie of doubting scholars engaged in abstract heterodox studies who use the Bible as a study tool. Nor is the Bible for a generation who prefer to believe their doubts and doubt their beliefs. Rightly speaking, the Bible is not just a literary text; it is a living record for those who seek to live in God.

We are strongly tempted today to depart from biblical truth because of our generation's fashions of thought. Our forebears challenged the world with the message of the Bible because they believed in the authority of God's word over the entire spectrum of human life. But the world today pushes us to challenge God's word. Presenting some laboratory results or archaeological discoveries, and waving the flags of globalization, abolition of poverty and the bringing of world peace through human rights, the world today demands that we join in the pursuit of these goals on its own terms. In response, we cringe with fear and swallow the world's goals and means as sacrosanct. Rather than challenging them by declaring and clarifying biblical goals for humanity, we turn on God's word to revise it!

Today, a bishop can sit secure on his throne in his diocese and claim that Jesus could never have been born of a virgin, nor could he have been resurrected bodily. His evidence? It is against natural science! I shudder at how we swallow such arguments. If science is to be capable of determining what God can or cannot do, science must first be able to determine (prove?) God's existence. If science cannot determine that God exists, then arguments about what God can or cannot do in terms of science are mere nonsense. The person who accepts science as the final authority and yet talks as though he believes in God must be in some confused state. Science is known empirically; God is known by faith. Science is limited to what is knowable by human beings; God is knowable to humans, but extends far beyond what we can know. Because God is supreme, sovereign, omnipotent, omniscient and omnipresent, he is not subject to scientific scrutiny.

Other Christians have been overly influenced by the all-important American question, "How many dollars?", and have swallowed the assumption that life is all about money. This has led them into what is wrongly called prosperity preaching. Such preaching is one of the most noxious poisons against genuine Christian faith. The number of casualties of this brand of falsehood throughout the world today is unimaginable.

We are always tempted to be unfaithful to God's word when we fail to take time to understand the purpose of Christ and the power and sovereignty of God. We are also tempted when we hope to force God to meet people at places they choose instead of radically challenging people to turn to God. Our struggles may also stem from our desire to receive the honour and accolades of those who cheer us on only when we make bold to discredit our God and take our stand against him.

> One of the greatest needs of the contemporary church is conscientious biblical exposition from the pulpit. Ignorance of even the rudiments of the faith is widespread. Many Christian people are immature and unstable. And the major reason for this sorry state of affairs is the paucity of responsible, thorough, balanced biblical preachers. The pulpit is not the place to ventilate our own opinions, but to unfold God's word. …
>
> Where are the young evangelical men and women, who are determined by God's grace to stand firm in Scripture, refusing to be swept off their feet by the prevailing winds of fashion, who are resolved to continue in it and live by it, relating the

Word to the world in order to obey it, and who are committed to passing it on, as they give themselves to the ministry of conscientious exposition?[2]

The reproaches and troubles we suffer today in the church and the increase in the number of swindlers who now do business running churches are largely because Bible preaching has been taken to the precipice of worldliness.

The Family Front

It has been said that it is more difficult to be a Christian at home than anywhere else, and I have not known a single Christian disagree. Why is it hard to be truly Christian at home? I think it is because it is the place of firsthand contact. The family is the place where we have to meet ever-growing demands with lean resources. We do not encounter those in our home only in the context of joyful assemblies. They are always there. Whether we are grouchy or joyful, we have to respond to them. In the home we do not enjoy the luxury of retreating before we have to make a response to someone we think has treated us unfairly.

It is easy to feel very disturbed by a member of the family, especially a spouse, who is making many demands or not showing enough understanding. It is very easy, too, to queue up behind the devil to accuse them and see their failures in the dark light of our imagination. What we should be doing is clasping their arms in ours and moving on together.

Do you still love your husband? The money he spends on you has greatly dwindled. There are kids in the home to take care of, and at his age he may no longer be doing all the extra work that he used to do to make more money.

Is your spouse no longer matching up to the women you meet at work each day? She used to be trim and smart, but that was years ago. She is no longer as attractive as she once was. Her demands have increased, and most of them are on behalf of your children or domestic needs. She seems overbearing in her demand that you reduce your social circle to

---

[2] John R. W. Stott, *The Contemporary Christian* (Leicester: InterVarsity Press, 1992), 171–172.

cut costs and create time for your family. Do you still love your wife? Whose voice is speaking against your spouse in your mind?

I can assure you that when our estimation of our loved ones is tinged with disgust, much of the problem stems from our perceptions. If we keep listening to the suggestions of the devil, the hatred that he nurtures will soon vent itself in anger and frustration. It will ultimately bring problems to our families and ourselves. Love is easier: it covers a multitude of wrongs and broadens our perception, making us more accommodating and encouraging of our spouses. It not only helps us cope well with circumstances, it also often helps our spouses and loved ones to improve beyond any point to which they could have been pushed by criticism and hatred. Love is the greatest!

Do you love your kids? This is not to be measured in terms of the money you are willing to spend on them. Do you also find time to sit on the floor with them and build them up through conversations? I lost my father when I was eleven years old. Today I am a man, but each time I look around and see kids wandering all over the place, I remember what great qualities my father bequeathed me by just sitting around with me. Few fathers would ever discipline their boys the way my father did me, but I still miss him as a great friend. It pains me that he is not around today to relish the result of his applying biblical principles in bringing up his children.

Many Christian parents today attend all manner of meetings – church meetings, business meetings, social meetings. But it is rare to find parents who enter into their kids' world, listen to them, and give themselves to be cherished and trusted by their kids. In fact, very few spend even five hours a week with their kids. Those who do spend time with them tend to spend it in stereotyped semi-formal prayer meetings. They also find time to scold their kids, or on occasions to talk to them about something they did. Yet such parents hope to raise Christian giants. They resort to sending their kids to all manner of Christian meetings, youth clubs, etc. These are important but only supplementary. The lives of the young are moulded at home.

Parental ministry is a very important part of our calling; in fact, home ministry ranks first. If we cannot bring up our own children, we have no business going to raise other peoples' children at church. We must give our kids time to gain confidence, self-esteem, values and a worldview by interacting with them and giving them attention. If we are not there to give them these things, they are likely to pick up contradicting values and wrong signals from others they meet outside the family. The formation of values in their hearts will then be flawed, leaving them unprepared to face later life. Some of them will be left immature, easily swayed by their friends' opinions.

Some parents pervert the home, so that it is the last place family members want to go when they are tired at the end of the day. This group includes women who constantly criticize their husbands, and men who demand of their wives such submission as is only due to God. Such uncompromising attitudes will boomerang in the long run. No sacrifice is too great to create a home that both parents and children want to rush back to at the end of the day.

These days everyone complains about the character flaws in modern teenagers. Of course, the situation is not always as bad as we paint it, for the generation gap sometimes leads us to exaggerate flaws. But many of the problems of which we complain should have been taken care of from infancy. Human character remains malleable until a certain age, and the Bible teaches, "Start children off on the way they should go, and when they are old they will not turn from it" (Prov. 22:6). Any evil parent may bring up evil children because he or she does not have good values to bequeath the kids. Yet righteous parents may also bring up unworthy children if they do not make time for them, but abandon them to grope around and be infected by any available value. Wonder what happened to Eli's children, Samuel's children and David's children? These were very busy men of God who may not have had time to spend with their kids. How could Samuel have spent time with them when he was sacrificing and judging Israel in a circuit of cities every year? (1 Sam. 7:15–8:3). With more than average exploits in war and his many wives, concubines and children, how could David ever have given due attention to his kids? God did not miraculously make these men's kids turn out well just because their parents were among his favourites. Parents must bring up their kids in the way they wish the kids to continue their lives (for children are extensions of their parents' lives). Those who do not care what their future on earth will be through their children can afford to ignore them.

Many parents have to run around sorting out their adult children in trouble just because they did not stay around when they should have. Many teenagers have turned to gangs and secret cults to find the love they should have found in caring homes. Yet the parents wonder where the reproach is coming from. Many young girls have eloped to love nests away from home. Their parents were never there when they were forming their characters, and now they have formed troubled characters that only God can change. Fixing their problems will take much more than all the money made, for which they were abandoned as kids. It will take much more attention than they needed when they were infants to guide them as adults. Even more, there is only sorrow in handling troubles for adults, instead of the joy of rightly bringing up kids.

Struggles on the home front are unlike other struggles. There is a demand that we provide money, and also a demand for the time we need to make the money. Our spouse and children will enjoy the benefits of being famous if our efforts bring them into the limelight, but building our families is not often the route to social acclaim. We have to face the struggle between building a home against all odds and wrecking it for today's pleasure. We can weather this struggle only as we look up to receive our strength from God.

And More …

This chapter has not dealt with all the practical issues with which Christians struggle. We have not even mentioned those who drive wedges between Christians, and those ministers who raise their flock by giving them a false sense of superiority over other Christians. There are others who still maintain the caste ideas related to race, gender or ancestry and uphold ancient caste laws that are manifestly unjust to others. In dealing with all such issues, we need to think of the people involved and consider the good of others.

In Matthew 22:37–40 Jesus tied together "Love the Lord your God" (Deut. 6:5) and "Love your neighbour as yourself" (Lev. 19:18). These two commandments are not to be separated. Actually, because none of us sees God in this life, it is only through obeying the second commandment, to love our neighbour, that we can manifest our love for God. So although our holiness relates to God, the evidence of our holiness relates to people. You cannot possibly love God and hate his image, regardless of how mangled and distorted the image may be. You can never love God and hate people he has made. The extent to which you are willing to go with God is reflected in the extent to which you are willing to go for others.

Our victory or failure in these struggles depends on our view of Jesus. How much of our lives are we giving to him who gave his life for us? If Jesus lives my life as I accept his values as mine, if my life is lived with recourse to Jesus, reflecting him to the society around me, then my struggles are as good as over. They will not last forever.

Questions

1. Which of the inner conflicts discussed in this chapter affect you personally?
2. What inner motives are behind your inner conflicts?
3. What would you suggest as ways through these conflicts?

8

BRIEF NOTES ON ENTANGLING SINS

Entangling sins are besetting sins. They are sins that recur despite our struggles against them. They are special case sins because they are deeply rooted in our personalities and have a strong capacity to entwine with our feelings of inadequacy, insecurity and emptiness to dominate certain areas of our lives. They tend to create the impression that they are legitimate hungers, feelings or responses to our inner needs. They access our reasoning, claiming that they are natural or inborn, so that we cannot extricate ourselves from them. And unless the reasoning patterns that induce and protect them are uprooted, these sin-cycles remain obsessive and shackling. The devil finds them useful in continuing his battle against our faith.

Sources of Entangling Sins

Entangling sins have many roots. Some stem from psychological pressures in our childhood, others from traumas or problems we have encountered as adults, and still others from imbalances in our own body chemistry.

Some people have grown up in homes where they were constantly ashamed of the way their parents behaved. Others, often those from polygamous homes, have had to compete for their parents' love and for almost every morsel of food. Those forced to become child soldiers have been warped by their early exposure to violence, mayhem, torture and rape, which were presented to them as heroic acts. Many handle these types of experiences by becoming loners or by resorting to drugs or alcohol. They often end up in some type of trouble.

We all know smokers who started the habit because of peer pressure, and drug users and alcoholics who started using these substances to numb their senses so that they would feel okay when they were with others. These people suffer from a sense of inadequacy and can only feel "normal" if their friends approve of them. Their condition may stem from an intimidated childhood. They may have had harsh and unappreciative parents – the type of parents who harshly criticize a child for only scoring 88 per cent because he ought to get higher grades. Or it may have been a teacher who constantly picked on the child and convinced him or her to think, "I am no good."

If you have talked to a pessimist, you may wonder why they are incapable of believing that anything good will come their way. It may be that their parents never believed in them. A pessimist can hardly ever accept a compliment. The last time the committee chairman commended the pessimist for presenting a very detailed report, she worried that she had been too verbose. You ask her to head a subcommittee, and she refuses, insisting it is beyond her abilities. You ask her to serve as an ordinary member, and she complains that nobody trusts her. She often misinterprets jokes. You have to be careful even when you smile, for she will claim you were making fun of her.

Some men started to visit bars in order to escape from nagging wives at home. There they met up with other men with similar problems. The place became a refuge, and the drinkers become their friends. Over time, they were drawn more and more into drinking to escape their troubles at home, and the acceptance and love of their drinking friends smoothed the path to alcoholism.

Some workaholics find security in the amount of work they can do. Others are motivated by an obsessive desire to accumulate wealth or own property. Still others slide into workaholism through working with user-friendly tools with which they establish a personal relationship. For example, computer users can come to relish the power of the computer and the thrill of discovering the undiscovered. Our culture is raising many computerholics who abandon their families for the thrills of the computer and the unlimited world of the Internet. Many stockbrokers suffer from the same problem. Even when they are with their families, their minds are elsewhere. They are constantly changing the radio or TV channel, hunting for news that may affect the market. Such workers keep setting up one target after another and their self-esteem depends on pursuing new targets.

Tackling Entangling Sins

The devil will try to convince you that you are worthless and that it is not even worth trying to break free of an entangling sin. Each time you struggle, or feel you are not progressing as fast as you would like, he will redouble his attacks. But all besetting sins can be uprooted by sincere love. Once you come to realize the problem, and recognize that there is One who is all powerful to help, you are in a position to start breaking free of their bondage. This deliverance may be slow, but your freedom will grow as you find the courage to allow Jesus into the innermost recesses of your mind and emotions and allow him to rummage through all the secrets hidden there.

Are you going to live by Jesus' principles and instructions? Will you forgive those who brazenly betrayed your love? The solution is not in forgetting about what was done or glibly offering forgiveness. You will need to review what exactly happened and take a positive step to forgive. Are you willing to love all others as you love yourself and enjoy free and sincere fellowship with Christians? If your answer is yes, then you are letting fresh air and light into the dark corners of your life.

It helps to know that your problem is not the other person. Your problem is your own reaction to the other person. You need to stop blaming them and see that it is self that is eating you up. It may help you to share your experience with a loving, caring and sincere person, preferably of the same gender as you. This should be someone you trust, with whom you can be fully open. You do not need to be ashamed of a fault you have admitted is wrong and which you are working hard to overcome. Find a mature Spirit-filled Christian to share your experience with. Ask an older, more spiritual and stable character to pray for you, monitor you, and encourage you as you set and review targets to escape your bondage.

Learn to love and feel loved. Circulate freely amongst believers and loved ones. Be careful not to slip into moods or take to heart peoples' remarks about you, for this can be severely destabilizing. You may just be subjecting yourself to harassment by someone else's skewed reaction due to their own entanglements. Taking people's opinions about us to heart is another way of swallowing Satan's distortion of our image. Once we take a wrong view of ourselves, we will start "misbehaving" in an effort to turn away from what is actually the right course for us, but which another person views wrongly. Let other people's assessments fall at the threshold of your heart. While considering their compliments or criticisms, do not let them affect your self-evaluation.

Rejoice always. Find reasons why you should be happy, especially because of the acceptance, forgiveness and help you receive from Jesus. Rejoice even if your efforts to escape your entanglement are only gradually yielding results, for that entanglement will not last for ever. To rejoice is one of the healthiest exercises for the mind.

Do not ever again start yielding to the temptation to replace relationships with objects or events. But don't do outlandish things to keep relationships going. Learn to trust God to help you do as much as you can rightly do. Do not give in to activities that continuously keep you away from others. Find reasonable leisure time for respected friends. Do not ever succumb to any pressure that will keep you away from fellowshipping and freely sharing with other Christians.

The following tables show some common features and suggested antidotes for some besetting sins. But treat the tables carefully. People are complex, and cannot simply be fitted into slots. Moreover there are often several factors at work and people may suffer from several besetting sins at once.

BESETTING SIN	PRIMARY CAUSES	PRIMARY PURPOSE OF VICTIM	SECONDARY MAINTAINERS	ANTIDOTE
GLUTTONY	Emptiness of heart due to non-fulfilling pursuits or relationships	To assuage the emptiness of the soul mistaken for emptiness of the stomach	Continued feeling of emptiness in heart	Filling your heart with a fulfilling and purposeful relationship, especially with Christ Counselling
SUBSTANCE ABUSE Alcohol, tobacco, hard drugs (e.g. marijuana, cocaine, heroin)	Peer pressure Sense of inadequacy Dysfunctional relationships Suppression of pain	To be accepted by peers To numb or heighten feelings To keep with people who share the same feelings Adventurism/rebellion	Sense of helplessness Continuation of primary cause Chemical addiction	Appreciating that the act is wrong Accepting that there is help in Jesus Letting go of old wrongs done to one Loving and being loved Christian counselling/ prayers Therapy
WORKAHOLISM	Self-imposed goals Environment Dysfunctional relationships Relationship with work tools/events	To exceed society's expectation of success To achieve a goal To experience the thrill of adventure To avoid unwanted relationships	Emotions associated with the first achievements Increasing love affair with tools or events Continued ill-feeling towards others	Reorientation so that you do not pursue results just for the thrill of the hunt or because it makes you stand out Replacing loved objects or events with persons

BESETTING SIN	PRIMARY CAUSES	PRIMARY PURPOSE OF VICTIM	SECONDARY MAINTAINERS	ANTIDOTE
LYING/ DECEPTION	Doing things we hate to be identified with Personality conflicts Fear	To impress people around us To deceive others for gain	Continued primary cause	Trusting and fearing God rather than people Being disciplined enough to try to do only the right thing Learning to own up and apologize if you are in the wrong
SEXUAL SIN	Pursuit of thrills, hedonism, and the deceptive promises of secret things Childhood-induced dysfunctional psychology A sense of victory gained by experiencing the objects of desire	To soothe the ego To escape other problems and be happy To enter a simulated world by being with the young, the beautiful, the smiling, or sometimes the weird, or simply with another human being	Initial denial by a loved one Continued primary causes	Facing the hard choice: your life or your thrill Unlearning the driving lies Rejecting secrecy Developing healthy sexuality Counselling

BESETTING SIN	PRIMARY CAUSES	PRIMARY PURPOSE OF VICTIM	SECONDARY MAINTAINERS	ANTIDOTE
BITTERNESS	A deep sense of betrayal by someone who was loved and trusted	To protect against any repetition of the primary negative event To blame oneself for being too trusting and thus feel good at the expense of those who are now denied love and trust	Withdrawal into a shell which shields the person from being reached by a releasing experience	Opening up and forgiveness Prayer and counselling
PESSIMISM	Timidity due possibly to early and sustained sense of failure imparted by others such as critical parents or teachers	To exercise complete caution in all life's affairs to avoid disappointment or shouldering the blame for anything else going wrong	Continuing self-image as a failure Rarely taking any risks, yet still assuming the need for even more cautious planning Anticipating failure in everything	Trusting God rather than your own carefulness for security Recognizing that under God you have an abundance of possibilities Counselling

BESETTING SIN	PRIMARY CAUSES	PRIMARY PURPOSE OF VICTIM	SECONDARY MAINTAINERS	ANTIDOTE
LONELINESS	Continually living among people from whom you are psychologically and socially separated (a pastor's sickness)	To maintain a dignified view of your profession or person	Continued non-participation at your real psychological and social level	Lightening the burdens of heart that no other has been permitted to share by genuinely and reasonably involving with your immediate environment and entrusting your personal and professional image to God
	Early rejection that creates difficulty in forming attachments	To avoid rejection	Pastors always on their toes to keep the ministry (God?) in honourable view	
REACTIVE ANGER	An emotive, unstable or superficial personality	On-the-spot reaction to feelings of disappointment	Superficial personality	Dealing with the primary cause
	Trauma from abuse (e.g. child abuse, rape, prostitution and addictions)	Psychological or mental disorder	Leaning too much on emotions rather than reason	Developing healthy thinking patterns and acting on the basis of reason, not just feelings
		Self-hate viewed as hate by others (a prostitute's disease)	Continued hatred of self-image	Putting absolute trust only in God and not in anyone else
				Forgiveness and love of self in line with God's love and forgiveness
				Therapy

Besetting sins are entangling, but they are progressively destroyed as the Holy Spirit reforms us. As we love, forgive, open up and completely trust God, their power is broken. The most potent power against besetting sins is the cross of Christ and the power of God at work in our lives. Our selfless surrender to God and growth in loving all others as ourselves, combined with our involvement in sincere loving relationships with others, are keys to our deliverance from these bondages.

Never think that you are the only one who is in bondage to such a sin. That is a devil's lie. Jesus said that everyone who sins is a slave of sin (John 8:34). Is a slave free? And how many of us did not give ourselves to sin before Jesus entered our lives to deliver us? Do not be ashamed; the enslaving principle is Satan's instrument against everyone, but now you can cooperate with Jesus and observe a new you emerge as Christ unties your shackles.

Don't give up! Jesus has conquered those entangling sins for you. He is letting you move into freedom progressively, as much as you can handle at a time.

Questions

1. What are entangling sins?
2. Which entangling sins affect your life?
3. Have you attempted to trace the root cause of your problem?
4. What does the author suggest you do to overcome your problem?

9

THE HOLY SPIRIT AND YOUR MIND

For more than two decades, the work of the Holy Spirit in guiding the believer has been avidly discussed. One result has been that some Christians now talk as if the Holy Spirit's guidance is the opposite to using our minds, or in other words, as if spirituality is opposed to reason. But we are told that we are to be transformed through the renewing of our minds (Rom. 12:2). What does this mean in practice? Does it not mean that once you have given your life to Christ, both your mind and the Holy Spirit matter?

The Holy Spirit Connection

When the Holy Spirit brings our spirits to life, he also charges us with the energy we need to get going. But if we do not recharge our spirits, we will run out of energy after a while. We need to maintain a proper link to the Holy Spirit to ensure that our spiritual batteries are constantly supplied so that we can function effectively.

This lesson was brought home to me very clearly one morning. I was stressed out because my car would not start, and I had to get to an early morning appointment. I could not understand what could have gone wrong. I had used the car the previous night without any problems. Tired and frustrated, I called in the auto-electricians. They soon identified the source of the problem – my car's battery was flat. The connection to the alternator had come loose, and the battery was not being charged. Without a stored electrical charge, the car's starter motor could not kick in, and the engine, the lights and horn would not work. Nothing would work properly until the battery was connected to a source of power and recharged.

The situation is the same in our spiritual lives. Many Christians are not functioning properly because they are not properly linked to the Holy Spirit. The devil is happy when we allow choir practice or business meetings to replace our regular private waiting on the Lord, where the Holy Spirit speaks to us personally and recharges us. Many of us have also allowed our quiet times to slide into dead routines with no sparks from on high to ignite our lives. The devil will do everything he can to cut us off from the Holy Spirit so that we are running on half-charged batteries.

Any Christian who wants to live well and make a mark for God must not forget to follow Jesus' example. He regularly took time off to go to a lonely place to pray and meditate, waiting to get instructions and spiritual refreshment from the Father (Mark 1:35; 6:46; Luke 11:1).

When we take time off to be alone with God studying the Scriptures, the Holy Spirit comes and brings the words of Scripture alive in our circumstances, thus renewing us and sharpening our vision. However, it is easy to rush through our reading fast, without waiting on the Lord. Our old nature will fight hard to discourage us from focusing fully on God without being distracted. But we must master the devil's gimmicks and hook up strongly to the Spirit.

When the Holy Spirit dwells fully in a believer, he produces a harvest of righteousness in that person's life. This inevitable harvest is "love, joy, peace, patience, kindness, goodness, faithfulness, gentleness and self-control" (Gal. 5:22–23). Under the influence of the Holy Spirit the believer will have the right attitude and disposition of mind to overcome the flesh and the devil.

Why Your Mind Matters

We sometime encounter believers who claim to depend on the Holy Spirit rather than reason. They imply that they have superior faith because they have switched off their rational minds and simply depend on extraneous promptings. But this type of talk is often no more than an excuse for a lack of proper training and planning. In fact, the belief that our minds are useless for our walk in Christ or inherently opposed to the Holy Spirit is a lie. The devil wants us to be mindless, non-thinking Christians. Mindless Christians are never spiritual Christians because when they give up their thinking faculty the devil is quite happy to take it over and play the role of an "angel of light".

We need to learn how we can work with both the Holy Spirit and our minds. A right thinking mind is not contrary to the Holy Spirit, nor is true reasoning contrary to faith. Our minds function as a clearinghouse. Whatever voices or factors speak to us (whether the Spirit, the flesh, self, or other people), all speak directly or indirectly to our mind. It is our mind that gives meaning to what we hear. It is also the mind that assigns weight to what we hear, so that we value different things differently. It is our mind's job to screen our thoughts and ideas to identify whether what we are hearing is genuine information that should be accepted as true and should give impetus to or restrain our actions. All our actions and inaction are direct products of our minds. It is thus important that we train our minds to perform this vital task well.

In all Jesus' dealings with people, we find him providing reasons for the actions he takes. He effectively used his mind while operating in line with the Holy Spirit's directions. For example, on one occasion he asked two questions: "What is written in the Law? ... How do you read it?" (Luke 10:26). His first question about what is written in the Scriptures was a question about what the Spirit says. His second question addressed how his listeners' minds interpreted what the Spirit says. Jesus calls us to train our minds so that we can interpret correctly what the Spirit is saying to us. We need to develop good minds in order to be able to separate genuine Christian faith from beliefs that come from culture, superstition and contemporary fashions of thinking. It is only when our minds are exposed to the light of truth that we can respond properly to the Holy Spirit.

If your mind understands what the Holy Spirit is saying, your mind will guide you correctly; but if your mind does not understand what the Holy Spirit is saying, you will be guided in wrong directions, even if you may think that you are being led by the Holy Spirit. We can easily make mistakes if we do not know how to distinguish between what the Holy Spirit is saying and what our own flesh is saying.

Christians can train their minds by personal systematic Bible study, as well as through Bible studies with church groups and non-denominational groups. It is also a good idea to read good, educative Christian literature and to listen to sound Christian teachers. They will sharpen our minds and help us to decipher the gimmicks and lies of the enemy.

It is also important to remember that the people's characters reflect their minds. When peoples' minds are pleased, they smile; when they are displeased, they frown. When somebody's mind is insensitive to the feelings of others, we describe the person as wicked. We know that somebody's mind is filthy when he or she says impure things. When someone's mind is deeply influenced by God, we say the person is godly, and when someone's mind is drawn to other people's plight, we say they are kind-hearted.

We are actually products of our minds, and thus our transformation to holy living can only be accomplished by the renewal of our minds. It is thus important that we train our minds to understand and value the Holy Spirit. We must also make time to really be with the Holy Spirit, studying with our minds and spirit under him. Our minds will then learn to value the things of God above the material things of this life, the honour of others, and our own selfish inclinations. Our minds must be taught to properly relate to the Holy Spirit by learning from him and obeying him as we regularly wait upon him to instruct us on how to live.

Questions

1. What role does the Holy Spirit play in helping us live the Christian life?
2. What role do you think the mind plays in our renewal?
3. How useful is your mind as an instrument of spirituality?
4. How can we make the best use of both our minds and the Holy Spirit?

10

THREE STEPS TOWARDS CHRISTIAN MATURITY

We have already learnt a lot about the struggles we face in this life. We must now take steps to minimize the areas of life in which we struggle and to improve our potential to win in the areas where there is still conflict. As we grow as believers, we will notice a change. Whereas we once struggled with things that were clearly sins, things like stealing and adultery, we come to struggle with more subtle versions of these same sins – like the temptation to borrow from others without repaying them or indulge in lustful thoughts. And so it will carry on, with the devil constantly coming up with more refined versions of temptation to play to the same basic desire. It is therefore necessary to learn how to constantly keep our minds pure and to beef up our spirituality in order to thwart his attacks.

Sin keeps calling to us, apparently oblivious to the fact that we have been snatched from its clutches. Our sinfulness extends from our outright sins, to our inability to do what we ought to do, to our vulnerability to things we ought not do. The cry sounds louder each day: "Who will rescue me from this body of death?" The answer only whispers, " – Jesus Christ our Lord!" (Rom. 7:24–25).

Through Jesus we have been rescued from bondage to sin. Through Jesus, too, we have been given power over sin. He did all that was necessary to liberate us from sin, with the result that heaven reckons us free of sin and full of righteousness. Each of us must now live out that righteousness here on earth. There are thus two sides to our struggle:

what Jesus did and what I now do by the help of his Spirit. In other words, there is God's role and my role.

So far, we have dwelt mostly on the efficacy of what God did in Christ Jesus to make us holy. We have been delivered from sin. But we need to understand what this means. Universalists point to descriptions of Jesus as "the Lamb of God, who takes away the sin of the world" (John 1:29) and argue that Jesus' sacrifice is universally efficacious. That is to say, his sacrifice avails for everyone who will ever tread this earth, regardless of whether they know about Jesus, believe in him, or even oppose his mission. They argue that God overlooks everyone's sin because Jesus has paid the price.

The power of sin is broken in the lives of those who have accepted the sacrifice of Jesus Christ for the salvation of their souls. But to say that sin's power is broken is not the same as saying that it no longer tries to influence our lives. It rather means that it has no more authority over those of us who have believed in Christ Jesus for their salvation. It is here, at the point of how the bondage of sin is broken, that the Universalists' arguments fail.

In chapter 2 we pointed to Isaiah's words as a key to understanding the nature of sin: "We all, like sheep, have gone astray, each of us has turned to our own way" (Isa. 53:6). We have not just followed paths we have chosen, but also selfish paths. And this is the root of sin: it pits us against God in the foolishness of our hearts, and it pits each of us against everyone else as we seek to get what we want. And it is this attitude that Jesus reversed by his sacrificial death. But it would not be reversed by his sacrificial death alone. The day he died the curtain of the temple was torn so that everyone could troop into the holiest of holy places, but millions still turned their backs to God. The Romans still oppressed the Jews, men still fought with other men, women were still discriminated against in the very heart of Jerusalem. Sin continued even though Jesus had died.

It is the second factor, our faith in his death, that really deals the cut. Jesus' death provides the sword and even sharpens it, but our exercise of faith in that sacrifice is what cuts the rope of bondage to sin.

How does it do that? The answer can be found in one of the metaphors Jesus used to describe Christian living: "Whoever wants to be my disciple must deny themselves and take up their cross daily and follow me"

(Luke 9:23). When we come to Christ in faith, our submission to him involves self-denial. It is the denying of self with its selfishness and pride and the surrender to God in repentance that breaks the power of sin in a believer's life. You kick self from the throne of your life and enthrone God as king. You turn from self-centeredness to God-centeredness. And thus the bondage to sin through self is broken. There is a deeper walk of self-denial to which the Lord Jesus calls us in discipleship, but this initial self-denial is what sets us on the path for discipleship.

It is this essential turning from self to God that Universalists gloss over when they make their claims. In reality, there is no salvation or taking away of anyone's sin, whether in principle or in practice, without a corresponding deliverance from bondage to self. From self-chosen ways we need to turn to God-appointed ways. From self-serving ways, we need to turn to altruism. Thanks be to God that the centrifugal force that tossed us all apart is broken. We are now drawn closer to one another as we come nearer and nearer to God as our epicentre. The yoke to self, which led to our discord with God and disharmony with one another, is broken. It is this turning of our hearts from self to God that is the breaking of the power of sin. On this ground every other thing about our elevation in holiness is achievable.

It is through Jesus Christ that we are rescued as we turn to him by faith in repentance from sin and take the daily practical steps towards him that keep us pure and strong in heart to engage in our daily endeavours to live holy lives. There are three such steps that will make us grow in practical holiness and erect strong defences against the temptations that come our way.

Step 1: Keep Your Eyes Fixed on Jesus

If we are to live in victory over sin, we need to keep our eyes fixed on the Lord Jesus Christ. The sinful nature still abides in us. The nearer our hearts are to the influence of sin, the more the sinful part of our heart is drawn to it and the more frequently and strongly it puts its pressure on us to compromise. But if we stay close to Jesus, we will be less likely to be so pressed.

Jesus the Lamb of God is also Jesus the Word of God. John makes this link more explicitly than any other Bible writer: "In the beginning was the Word, and the Word was with God, and the Word was God" (John 1:1). "The Word" is more than just a mere title for Jesus. The author of Hebrews shows that it also means verbal expression when he opens his letter with the words, "In the past God spoke to our ancestors through the prophets at many times and in various ways, but in these last days he has spoken to us by his Son" (Heb. 1:1–2). Note the ways he says this: God spoke to us *through* prophets, but he has now spoken *by* his Son. God's message to us is his Son. Everything we see of him and hear from him is God's message to us. And God *has spoken;* he is not going to add to what has been said by the Son.

Jesus said, "The words I have spoken to you – they are full of the Spirit and life" (John 6:63). The Word of God is powerful in injecting and activating spiritual life, quickening our feeble and frail minds to engage in the struggles and stand against the temptations we face, especially those which encourage us to give up our faith. God has spoken through Jesus. His life, his deeds, and words are now recorded for us to live by. In him we have been given everything that we need for life and godliness. God has communicated his love for us, his work for our redemption, and our way of escape in Jesus Christ. It is now our responsibility to turn to Jesus and receive our food for life.

One often quoted statement of Jesus is "Then you will know the truth, and the truth will set you free" (John 8:32). In other words, the more you know the truth, the more you are freed from sin. But like Pilate we may still ask, "What is truth?" The answer is no secret: "I am … the truth" (John 14:6), said Jesus. He is the truth we can know, and he is the truth that sets us free as we know him.

But what does it mean to "know" Jesus? In New Testament times, the word "know" had a deeper and more intense meaning than it does today, when it tends to refer to knowledge gained second-hand or by passive inspection. Then, "to know" something meant that one had actively experienced it, and that this interaction had yielded a deep understanding. So what the passage tells us is that we will begin to enjoy the freedom that Jesus bought for us on the cross as we interact with him, engaging with him spiritually and mentally and thereby experiencing him. As we come to know him, he sets us free from sin.

The knowledge of Jesus has a similarly liberating and empowering effect on our spirits. Jesus Christ is "a life-giving spirit" (1 Cor. 15:45).

As we look at Jesus, the life and truth he radiates into us systematically liberate us in our different areas of bondage and empower us to earnestly engage the flesh instead of submitting to it, as we did in fear when we were deceived by Satan's lies.

One of my own liberating experiences came the day I understood that the devil I had grown to dread as a powerful force warring against the Christ in me was created by my Christ. The devil is one of all those things, "visible and invisible … thrones or powers or rulers or authorities" over which Jesus Christ my Lord has active supremacy (Col. 1:16). Since that day, I have no longer been scared of what the devil can do to me or that he might steal my faith. I now see that Jesus is in full control. So when I take a look at the Lord Jesus Christ, I am empowered to take my stand for him.

What do you see when you look at Jesus? Some see Jesus as a very good teacher. To some, reeling under oppressive governments, the liberation theologians show Jesus as the leader who may even use armed struggle to escape misrule. To others he is synonymous with the law. Those who see Jesus in this light often fear that they are condemned. But Jesus is not the law; you need only come to him in faith and obedience now and he will be your Saviour. He himself said, "God did not send his Son into the world to condemn the world, but to save the world through him" (John 3:17).

What do Christians see when they look at Jesus? He "has become for us wisdom from God – that is, our righteousness, holiness and redemption" (1 Cor. 1:30). He looks quite different from what I see when I look at the law. The law shouts at me "you are unable to keep me and so you are condemned"; Jesus says to me, "There is now no condemnation for those who are in Christ Jesus". The law says to me, "Even your righteous acts are like filthy rags before God." But I see Jesus, who knew no sin, becoming sin for me that I might become the righteousness of God in him. The law says to me, "you fall short of the glory (that is, the holiness) of God"; Jesus says, "I give you power to become a child of God". The law says, "the wages of your sin is death"; Jesus says, "the gift of God is eternal life". So Christians see Jesus as their help, the one who has come to save them and not the one who condemns them. Jesus is the Christian's righteousness; he is the Christian's claim to heaven. He is our redemption.

I am empowered when I hear my Saviour say that he will not leave me alone in my struggles. He says that no matter how difficult things are, no matter how lonely I feel, he is there with me. No matter what public opinion weighs me down, I hear the voice of my Lord telling me to look to him and the city above and keep my act in line with the traditions of heaven.

When I see my Saviour, I see the pattern of what I ought to be. His image challenges me, and his strength in me urges me not to despair because of the difference between who he is and who I am. His Spirit empowers me to move towards him, one step at a time. No matter how shaky my step, no matter how imperfect my gait, the Holy Spirit uses it to make me more and more like him.

Jesus prayed to the Father, "Sanctify them by the truth; your word is truth" (John 17:17). One looks at Jesus by hearing and studying the word of God. The Holy Spirit of God, put in one at conversion, uses the word one hears and studies and the testimony of other believers to create in one a living knowledge of the Lord Jesus. It is by this word that the Holy Spirit imports into one's heart the portrait of the living Christ. One develops a greater capacity to receive more strength from Jesus as one obeys and conforms to what one sees of Christ.

Christians have long been encouraged to make time to study the word of God and to pray regularly. Most Christian groups encourage their members to make quiet moments for personal study of God's word on a daily basis. However, new believers may need more than a daily quiet time to grow and be well established. We need to feed and shore up our knowledge of Christ consistently and constantly, whether we are involved in an immediate struggle or not. This is the way to be sanctified and made holy. In fact, the things learnt of Christ will help me avoid potential struggles. So I need to fill my heart with the knowledge of him that comes by looking at him. I should keep my eyes glued on Jesus and keep focused on aiming to be like him. He is the highest prize to be won in this life.

What I see as I study the word of God or hear as others speak the word is of utmost importance in my spiritual growth. Many lessons are to be learnt from Scripture, but the key to speedy and stable growth is to relate all I learn to Jesus Christ in such a way as to see him as my model in all things. I also have to rely on him to supply all the strength needed to meet demands made on me or to overcome challenges thrown at me as I imitate my role model. I need to remind myself, "I can do all things through Christ that strengthens me", and trust him to sanctify me using his word as I study it.

My looking at Jesus is not something I can do just once. I have to carry on looking at him for the rest of my life because I need to become like him, exactly conformed to his image. I find that as my circumstances change, my need of Jesus increases. My hope is that I "be found in him, not having a righteousness of my own that comes from the law, but that which is through faith in Christ" (Phil. 3:9). In this life I never grow strong enough to become independent in any sense. I am only empowered to be a conqueror by continually looking at Jesus. He is the bread of life who promised, "the one who feeds on me will live because of me" (John 6:57).

Instead of spending all our time worrying about our struggles or some mistake or another, we should spend that time, and more, learning to understand who Jesus really is for us. That is the indirect but surest way of living victoriously.

The more we look at him the more we live like him. We need to keep our eyes fixed on him. Our different temperaments, dispositions and circumstances will try to create distractions so that we look away. But if we keep our gaze on him, we will find that while our circumstances change, we will continue to reflect him. We are empowered to be like him by looking at him.

Step 2: Cultivate a New Desire

"Those who live according to the sinful nature have their minds set on what that nature desires; but those who live in accordance with the Spirit have their minds set on what the Spirit desires" (Rom. 8:5). Looking at Jesus creates in us a desire to be like him. It is a question of where one's mind is. Have you seen a Christian live in a way that is pleasing to God? It is because the person's mind is set on becoming like Christ. This desire is far more powerful than any desire to keep God's law. The more we pursue keeping the law and strive to obey it, the more powerful it is at its own game of condemning us. But righteousness comes by grace. We are forgiven once we accept Jesus.

The immediate work of the Spirit after our justification is to seal us. "He anointed us, set his seal of ownership on us, and put his Spirit in our hearts as a deposit, guaranteeing what is to come" (2 Cor. 1:21–22). What does "guaranteeing" mean? A guarantee is an assurance of something, and in this case it is an assurance of the certainty of an expectation. There are two senses in which the Spirit is God's guarantee of our salvation. First, by guaranteeing God's promise to us, he assures us that God has already granted us entrance to his kingdom; God will not change his mind about it. This assurance encourages us to keep focused on Jesus instead of panicking with frustration when we fail to meet the demands of the law. Having now given us a token of the kingdom to come, he assures us that the kingdom will eventually be ours in full. Secondly, by ensuring that our faith in God remains, the Spirit guarantees that we will gain the kingdom. He does this by making us desire the life of Jesus and thus creates a hunger to conform to his image. He works in us to ensure that we do not get despondent and is ever whetting our desire for Jesus. In us, then, Jesus is alive because of the Spirit. We do not just know about Jesus in our heads, but we intimately relate with him because the Spirit imports him into our hearts. We live with the reality of a Saviour who is alive.

The Spirit's revelation of Jesus to our hearts is not passive but active. The knowledge of Jesus he brings creates in us a hunger to be like him. As the Apostle Paul says, "we … groan inwardly as we wait eagerly for our adoption, the redemption of our bodies" (Rom. 8:23). We long to be completely like him. This new desire for Christ displaces the old desires for carnal and material things. It gives birth to holy living.

When my sinful nature kept me valuing the things of this world, I clung to those things, gratifying myself with sin. But now my values have changed. I desire to love even those who hate me because that is what I see my Lord doing; I desire to be at peace with everyone, and to be patient with those who accuse me wrongly; I desire to be kind even in my assessment of those who speak evil of me and to be good to those who mistreat me. As I see Jesus, I desire to be gentle even when I am in the right. I also apply self-control in an attempt to be like my master. This desire tilts my struggles in the favour of righteousness. By looking at him, a new desire is created in me. Like the Apostle Paul, I "want to know Christ – yes, to know the power of his resurrection and participation in his sufferings, becoming like him in his death, and so, somehow, attaining to the resurrection from the dead" (Phil. 3:10–11).

When we turn and keep looking at Jesus and start desiring to be like him, something refreshing starts happening in us. The Apostle Paul caught this when he wrote; "Now the Lord is the Spirit, and where the Spirit of the Lord is, there is freedom. And we all, who with unveiled faces contemplate the Lord's glory, are being transformed into his image with ever-increasing glory, which comes from the Lord, who is the Spirit" (2 Cor. 3:17–18). When we enter into the presence of the Lord, we are liberated from our fear of and bondage to sin. And as we keep our gaze on the Lord, the Spirit of the Lord progressively transforms us to ever-closer approximations of his likeness. So the more we desire the Lord's glory, his person, his righteousness, his power, and his love, the more we are transformed into his likeness with ever-increasing glory, as the Holy Spirit works in us. It is our growth in the knowledge of Christ and the intensity of our desire for him that the Holy Spirit uses to charge our spiritual batteries to enable us to overcome temptations. This is the New Testament approach to practical holy living.

By focusing our attention on Jesus, the Spirit creates in us a hunger and thirst to be like him. This is the blessedness of the fourth beatitude. "Blessed are those who hunger and thirst for righteousness, for they will be filled" (Matt. 5:6).

The beatitudes teach the blessedness of the lifestyle that will grow in us as we feed on Jesus and yield to the sanctifying work of the Holy Spirit. The character traits that Jesus praises are ones that most people would turn their backs on as reserved for the unfortunate. I cannot acquire them by, for instance telling myself, "I want to be meek" and then watching each moment of my interaction with others. I would end up frustrated both by my inability to continue to show meekness and by the provocation to match the people around me in their own pride. Who would ordinarily want to accept poverty of spirit, or to be meek among their peers? Who would see any virtue in hungering after righteousness while others hunger after fun and pleasure? Who would want to be despised because of preaching the gospel? But Jesus points to the blessedness of these marks, the real pointers to our being part of the kingdom of God, because we acquire them as the Holy Spirit remoulds us by what we see and desire of Jesus. Others who do not see Jesus cannot have these qualities. They may pretend to have them, but they cannot have them from the inside. Many others cannot even see why one should even desire these qualities. However, when one sees Jesus, one sees their beauty and begins to long for them. In short, as we see Jesus live a spiritual life in the midst of glaring provocations, contentions and temptations, we abandon all carnality to pursue spiritual goals. But we could never react this way on our own. It is the act of the Holy Spirit to use what we desire of Jesus to make us like him.

Step 3: Act Out Your Faith

What proportions of faith and work are needed to carry us to ultimate redemption has always been a topic of argument. It is interesting that the apostle of faith, Paul, who unequivocally stated "it is by grace you have been saved, through faith – and this is not from yourselves, it is the gift of God – not by works, so that no one can boast" (Eph. 2:8–9) was also the one who instructed believers to "continue to work out your salvation with fear and trembling" (Phil. 2:12). Should we be like some liberal theologians and simply dismiss this as a clear pointer to the contradictory theological positions of a beclouded, ambivalent generation? Or should we dig deeper to find the inner truth in both positions? If we do, we will find that each becomes a defining quality of the other. James helps us understand this because he reconciles both positions in his epistle. He makes it clear that Christianity demands human responsibility built on the solid foundation of God's forgiving mercy and uplifting grace. Without this foundation one cannot stand, but on this foundation each one is expected to "put on the full armour of God, so that when the day of evil comes, you may be able to stand your ground, and after you have done everything, to stand" (Eph. 6:13).

It is very interesting to compare Galatians 5:22–23 and 2 Peter 1:5–11. Galatians speaks of the fruit of the Spirit; the result of the indwelling presence of the Holy Spirit. This is the side of the gift – the outworking of the promise on the basis of our faith, "for it is God who works in you to will and to act in order to fulfil his good purpose" (Phil. 2:13). We have stressed the fact that the foundation of our salvation and subsequent sanctification is laid on "grace through faith", comes by "promise not works", and is a "gift not merit". But we have not preached the full gospel unless we also stress the other side, that is, our responsibility to cooperate with the Holy Spirit in working out our growth in holiness. We are to "continue to work out [our] salvation with fear and trembling" (Phil. 2:12), and to "purify ourselves from everything that contaminates body and spirit, perfecting holiness out of reverence for God" (2 Cor. 7:1).

We see this pattern worked out in 2 Peter 1. In verse 3 Peter insists that we have been given "everything we need for a godly life through our knowledge of him who called us by his own glory and goodness." Thereafter, from verses 5 to 11, the apostle calls us to "make every effort" to ensure our ever-increasing sanctification. The issues he raises are ones that are important for us to work on. But as we do so, we need to remember that these efforts are based on what we have been given through our knowledge of the Lord.

Peter wrote, "make every effort to add to your faith goodness; and to goodness, knowledge; and to knowledge, self-control; and to self-control, perseverance; and to perseverance, godliness; and to godliness, mutual affection; and to mutual affection, love" (2 Pet. 1:5–7). Most of these qualities sound quite familiar. They are very similar to the fruit of the indwelling Holy Spirit Paul described in Galatians 5:22–23. Peter's point is that we are to work out the full manifestation in our lives of qualities already given us. We are to make an effort to live out the qualities that result from the operation of the indwelling Holy Spirit.

These principles can only be solidly efficacious if they are worked at on the basis of a life yielded in complete trust to the Lord Jesus Christ. We must take pragmatic steps consistent with the faith we have in Jesus to ensure the continuity and productivity of our faith. We should focus on acting like Jesus would, in faith that the Spirit within has granted us the necessary reformation to enable us to do so. There is no other way to discover the potential within and to use it. When provoked, for instance, I should not wait for a voice from above to tell me I have been granted self-control before I act with self-control. I should take the step of faith by acting as I know Jesus would. My step of faith will be imperfect, but it will help me know where I fall short, and will lead me to desire more of Jesus and to pray to be conformed to his image. As I do this, I become more like him.

Peter urges us to show the following qualities:

- **Goodness:** We are to make conscious efforts to be good to others. The rule that governs our attitude in this area is the Lord's instruction, "in everything, do to others what you would have them do to you" (Matt. 7:12). But this is easier said than done. It takes real effort to be really good to others, especially when these others may have been unjust to us, or are guilty of wickedness and blatant sin. Our natural tendency is to oppose them. But we are here instructed to actively do them good. We are not to wish them evil or plot their fall, even if they are not holy men. We should also do our best to see that they come to a saving knowledge of the Lord. When we position ourselves to be good to others including those who have wronged us, there will be no room to accommodate revenge. Nor is it enough to simply ignore unresponsive and unfriendly neighbours – on the basis of our faith in the Lord, we should actively demonstrate goodness here on earth. We should not see our faith as only a heavenly or spiritual affair; we should reflect the goodness of heaven to the world around us. We cannot afford to stand aloof.

- **Knowledge:** When we have made efforts to be good to our neighbours, we should add knowledge to this virtue. What do we have to know? We should make efforts to know in real terms why we believe what we believe and "be prepared to give an answer to everyone who asks [us] to give the reason for the hope that [we] have" (1 Pet. 3:15). We should understand the faith, and this will lead us to truly understand the world we live in so that our goodness does not stem from our ignorance of the world around us. Our goodness should stem from the benevolence of the magnanimous God who does not desire the death of a sinner but wants them to turn to him and live. We should know Jesus, not just in our heads but in our hearts as we experience his power in prayer and as we apply his word. To this firm knowledge of what we believe and why, we should add a good knowledge of the real world around us. This will make it difficult for us to be deceived by the gimmicks of the devil and less likely to swallow the ever-shifting opinions of the world. If we know the God of heaven, it will be difficult for even the most powerful of men to intimidate us. By adding knowledge to our goodness, we will be dealing with our inner struggles relating to societal values, public opinion, the assurance of our salvation, the efficacy of faith in Jesus Christ, and our reaction when we fall into sin.

- **Self Control:** There is a common saying, "Knowledge is power". The Bible puts it somewhat differently, "Knowledge puffs up" (1 Cor. 8:1). There is a danger that having knowledge will make us feel superior to others. As children of God, we may glory in our knowledge of the God of heaven and in our understanding of the workings of the powers, cultures and supercultures in which we live. But in our daily experience, we will face situations where we will be tempted to use what we know to achieve our own ends. That is why we need to add self-restraint to our knowledge. Mere knowledge may also not help us in emotional circumstances, where what is called for is self-control to ensure that we keep ourselves within the context of the kingdom lifestyle. Self-restraint helps us to consider not just the theoretical issues at play in a situation, but also the other people involved, who will be affected by our decisions or actions. That is why the Apostle Paul was prepared to say, "if what I eat causes my brother or sister to fall into sin, I will never eat meat again, so that I will not cause them to fall" (1 Cor. 8:13). Knowledge may help me know the extent to which I am at liberty in Christ, but this knowledge should be supplemented with self-control so as not to inadvertently destroy the faith of others while enjoying my liberty. Self-control helps in moderating my excesses, which could lead me into avoidable contradictions of my faith. Self-control helps me to say no when all the fleshly faculties in me say yes.

- **Perseverance:** With all the faith we have in God, all the goodwill we have towards others, all the understanding of life both spiritual and temporal, and all the self-restraint we are applying to ensure we do not rock the boat, we still need perseverance. Life will at times look sluggish and appear meaningless. We may either slide into depression or become aggressive; but the quality that is needed most at such times is perseverance. When things appear not to be working the way they should; when we have prayed and yet answers are slow in coming; when we have put the best into life yet seem to be reaping the wrong results; when it seems that hell is let loose against us and no one around seems to understand us, we can end up like Elijah, frustrated and besieging the Lord with complaints and confused demands to be taken home. In such situations a virtue we need ever so dearly is perseverance. Wait on the Lord, try and get sleep, learn not to be overwhelmed by whatever visible evidence is about to dislodge your faith. Wait, the Lord must surely show himself faithful. It does not matter how horrible your battle is, how bleak the prospects, close your eyes and say no to what is wrong. Learn the attitude of not despairing; never consider the possibility of giving in to what is wrong because of tomorrow. Persevere! You will be elated you did when the contention is over.

- **Godliness:** Godliness is living our life moment by moment in view of God. It is a quality that rubs off on one as one meets with God. It does not have any special apparel, although one very potent temptation of spirituality is to pretend it does. To show by what one wears, eats or by one's idiolect that one is spiritual is a superfluous hindrance to true godliness. Godliness is the conduct or posture of spirituality. It is an attitude of firm and living faith in God. In the eyes of godly people we see sincerity, in their voices we decipher the serenity that passes understanding, in their faces we observe knowledge of the assurance of God's presence. Godliness stems from secret interactions with God in prayer, not from public statements of belief. Godliness is the necessary attitude of a yielded life immersed in the study of and obedience to scriptural truth. Godliness is the quality of a life completely surrendered to God.

- **Mutual Affection:** We must make an effort to be large-hearted towards others. This applies as much to the opinions we hold of others as to the gifts we give them. We should endeavour to be kind in our assessment of others, and kind in dealing with them. Spiritual people can be unkind towards those they disagree with. Sin has warped the world around us, and encourages us to stand aloof and close our eyes to it. But we must make deliberate efforts to show kindness to others in our different contexts, to meet with them in their hurting circumstances, and by the grace of God offer the balm of Gilead. If we have a kind disposition, we will see many people's proud, boastful and competitive spirits as symptoms of a perishing generation. We should then be kind enough to launch out for them instead of making more laws that will only keep them away from us and soothe our own egos.

- **Love:** Love is the crowning quality we must endeavour to add to our faith and to all the other virtues that flow from it. We may be surprised at being told to make an effort to love, because it is often thought that love is an indeterminable emotional reaction towards others. Nothing could be farther from the truth. Love is cultivated; it can also be stirred up. We are called to make every effort to crown our faith with love. The surest way to love others is to see them in the same light God sees them. His love led him to pay the supreme price for them. Love may also require that we adjust our opinions of them. We must love others; that is to say, we must be charitable in our disposition towards them.

Peter gives two key reasons why we need make these efforts. These have been discussed at length in chapter 5, and thus we will only briefly touch on them here.

First, Peter says, "If you possess these qualities in increasing measure, they will keep you from being ineffective and unproductive in your knowledge of our Lord Jesus Christ" (2 Pet. 1:8). Our growth in sanctification will ensure our fruitfulness in Christ Jesus. There is no other way to be an effective ambassador of Christ, turning other souls to the knowledge of him, and being useful in building up the faith of those who have already turned to Christ, despite the inner battles that confront us.

His second reason is that we should "make every effort to confirm your calling and election. For if you do these things, you will never stumble, and you will receive a rich welcome into the eternal kingdom of our Lord and Saviour Jesus Christ" (2 Pet. 1:10–11). Our faith in Christ needs moment by moment maintenance; we cannot afford to run dry even if just for a moment, for that could spell disaster. But if we live out these qualities, we will not fall. Our faith in Christ will continually blossom, and thus we will receive a rich welcome into our eternal home.

Looking to Jesus, desiring to be like him, and acting on what we know are the three steps we must take to keep our spiritual batteries charged so that we can overcome the inner struggles that draw us to compromise our faith and quit. We look at Jesus by constantly studying the Scriptures and meditating on him. We must create quiet moments to study, meditate and pray. Doing this regularly will build up enormous strength for us. In prayer, we must request to be conformed to the image of Jesus, our desire. The Holy Spirit within keeps reforming us to become like what we desire. And then we act in two ways: the first is the positive action of constantly relating to the world around us with the mind of Christ, which we now live by. The second is by engaging in all our life endeavours and struggles secure in our knowledge of Christ, so that we know how to handle temptations that come our way and, when we fail, know to rise up and go back to Christ.

On no grounds should I consider compromising my faith or quitting it. If in my striving to become like Jesus I fail at some point, the answer is not to give up the struggle and adopt lower standards, being deceived that I cannot become more like Christ, or that failure is natural to me. No, God is working in us to make us like Jesus. Do not give up. God is already at work in you. Do not let an evidence of your failure draw you away. God has never failed; he will not fail in you. Arise again in Christ and ask for more grace to rise to the heights of walking with God. Reach out again for those great aspirations you once had to know him. As you aspire to those heights, sin will always try to discourage you, but Jesus said, "whoever comes to me I will never drive away" (John 6:37).

Questions

1. List the three steps that charge our spiritual batteries.
2. How does the Holy Spirit whet our desire for Christ?
3. How does the Holy Spirit use our desires and obedience to build up our inner strength and values?
4. In what area of your life do you have to improve to ensure you win this battle of faith?